Angel Answers

Also by Andrew Ramer

Ask Your Angels (*coauthor*)

The Spiritual Dimensions of Healing Addictions (*coauthor*)

Further Dimensions of Healing Addictions (*coauthor*)

little pictures

Two Flutes Playing

Tools for Peace

For orders other than by individual consumers, Pocket Books grants a discount on the purchase of **10 or more** copies of single titles for special markets or premium use. For further details, please write to the Vice-President of Special Markets, Pocket Books, 1230 Avenue of the Americas, New York, NY 10020.

For information on how individual consumers can place orders, please write to Mail Order Department, Paramount Publishing, 200 Old Tappan Road, Old Tappan, NJ 07675.

Angel Answers

A JOYFUL GUIDE
TO CREATING
HEAVEN ON EARTH

Andrew Ramer

POCKET BOOKS

New York   London   Toronto   Sydney   Tokyo   Singapore

An *Original* Publication of POCKET BOOKS

POCKET BOOKS, a division of Simon & Schuster Inc.
1230 Avenue of the Americas, New York, NY 10020

Library of Congress Cataloging-in-Publication Data

Ramer, Andrew.
    Angel answers : a joyful guide to creating heaven on earth /
Andrew Ramer.
      p. cm.
   ISBN: 0-671-52589-1 (pbk.)
     1. Angels—Miscellanea. 2. Spiritual life. 3. New Age movement.
I. Title.
BF1623.A53R36   1995
291.2'15—dc20   94-47419
                                                        CIP

First Pocket Books trade paperback printing April 1995

10 9 8 7 6 5 4 3 2 1

POCKET and colophon are registered trademarks of
Simon & Schuster Inc.

Cover design by Christine Van Bree
Cover art and part-title art by Karen Haughey

Printed in the U.S.A.

ANDREW'S DEDICATION

To Barbara Grace Shor, archaeologist of the soul, for reintroducing me to Sargolais, and for a dozen years of friendship, exploration, and dancing with angels;

Dr. Irene Eber, who twenty-five years ago in a college classroom said six words that changed my life: "The body is the bodhi tree;"

the late Rabbi Max J. Routtenberg, who taught me as a child that more important than having the right answers is knowing how to ask the right questions

SARGOLAIS'S DEDICATION

To you, dear reader, created in joy, who are the future of this Earth and the hope of all the angels

The author would like to thank all of the people who worked on co-creating this book:

Editor · Emily Bestler
Editorial assistant · Amelia Sheldon
Agent · Howard Morhaim
Agent's assistant · Alison Mullen
Associate Copy Chief · Phyllis Braun
Free-lance Copywriter · Mary Mintzer-Kraushar
Managing Editor · Donna Ruvituso
Copyeditor · Cecilia Hunt
Director of Copyediting · Joann Foster
V.P./Director of Production · Irene Yuss
Production Manager · Lynda Castillo
Production Editor · Al Madocs
Book Designer · Stanley S. Drate
Executive Art Director · Paolo Pepe
V.P./Director of Subsidiary Rights · Dona Chernoff
V.P./Director of Marketing · Helene Atwan
Publicity Director · Liz Hartman
V.P./Director of Sales and Marketing · Lisa Rasmussen
Assistant Director of Publicity · Cindy Ratzlaff
Cover art and drawings · Karen Haughey
Proofreader · Scott Heim
The people at Quebecor/Fairfield, who printed this book

Contents

Part One
ALIGNING YOUR THOUGHTS
WITH YOUR SOUL

Part Two
ATTUNING YOUR THOUGHTS AND YOUR FEELINGS

Part Three
Awakening Your Body to Joy

AFTERWORD

Andrew's
Foreword

This is a handbook for living in a new millennium. It's a guide for transmuting ourselves from fearful, limited, destructive beings into the radiant children of God that we are.

For thousands of years angels have been coming into our world to herald change. Abraham, Sarah, Moses, Mary, Jesus, Mohammed, and Joan of Arc were all visited by angels. Today angels are coming to ordinary people in all walks of life. According to *Time* magazine, sixty-nine percent of Americans believe in the existence of angels and thirty-two percent have personally felt an angelic presence. What grand transformation are all of these angels announcing with their presence?

And—what is an angel? The word means *messenger* in ancient Greek. According to our scriptures, angels are messengers of God. To the mystics, angels are the image of our Perfect Self. Many of us think of them as beings of light. To a scientist an angel might be called, simply, a coherent information field.

As a boy I was fascinated by pictures of angels. But it never occurred to me that they were real—until the night in 1982 when one appeared in my bedroom. It was about seven feet tall, with golden hair, golden eyes, and enormous golden wings. Floating several inches above the floor, it walked toward me, put its hands on my shoulders, and pushed me down on my back, flooding my body with waves of pure love.

Each night for several weeks that angel, who called itself Gabriel, returned to talk to me and teach me. Each night it was a little less solid, till all that remained was its voice, still glowing in the bottom of my brain. My life was changed by the love that came to me from Gabriel and the angels who followed. They helped me to remember that angels had always been speaking to me, from the time I was small. And they let me know that angels are talking to all of us, all the time—but nobody teaches us to listen.

In 1987 Sargolais, my own guardian, or companion, angel, came into my life, in a field of pulsing golden light. More intimate than a lover, more constant than any other teacher, his presence has been in my awareness ever since that time, comforting, supporting, encouraging, inspiring, and guiding me. In the middle of the night, on the subway, on airplanes, I can be found with pen in hand, listening, questioning, writing down his answers.

Shortly after I met Sargolais, a mutual friend introduced me to Timothy Wyllie and Alma Daniel, who were also talking to angels and teaching others how to. Together the three of us wrote *Ask Your Angels*, a guidebook on how to start communicating with the angels and working with them in your life.

Angel Answers is the next step. It includes all the advanced material from Sargolais that did not go into *Ask Your Angels*. This book is a guide for listening, not just to the angels, but to the highest wisdom you carry within your heart. It's the next step in your journey toward living fully and the answer to my deepest and most often asked question: "Who are we, Sargolais, and why are we here?"

In a hundred years, our winged friends tell me, talking with angels will be ordinary. Allow yourself to imagine that world, and know that you are a vital part of its creation.

How to play in this book

This is a guide for becoming fully human. The angels haven't come into our lives so that we can bask in their divine light. They have come to help us see our own luminous beauty.

Angel Answers is a mirror in which to see all of who you are. It has three sections, each of which will support you in another area of your personal growth. In the first section there are messages from the angels that will align your thoughts and your soul. In the second, there are exercises to support you in attuning your emotions with your thoughts. In the third section you will find processes that will nurture your spiritual evolution on a physical, cellular level.

This is a book for *playing* in, not working with. Wander through it. Explore the sections you feel drawn to. Put it aside for months at a time. Come back to it later. There is no "right" way for you to use this book. Open it and see what you find. Sargolais and his angel friends wrote it to help you in your journey to God. There are many ways to get there, for God is ever-present, everywhere.

The angels have told me that all the religions of our world are different organs in its spiritual body. When you see the word *God* in this book, know that Sargolais is using it to speak of the One who created our universe, the Mother-Father Parent of us all.

When Sargolais suggested that I put together all the messages I had received from the angels, I was mad. It meant going through seven years of pads, computer disks, and twenty-three volumes of my journal, separating the passages meant only for me from the ones that belonged to everyone.

I thought it would take me six months to copy everything into my computer. It took three weeks. What a teaching that was! Rather than being a struggle, it was joyous and easy. Each section fell right into place. And I can still hear the angels' delicious laughter—when I realized that they had been writing this book all along.

As you play your way through ANGEL ANSWERS, please remember that every day can be joyous and easy for you too—when you open to the angels, and when you awaken to your birthright as a beloved child of God, here to participate in the creation of Heaven on Earth.

Sargolais's Foreword

At this time in your history you are preparing yourselves for a way of living on this planet that will be as transformational as when your distant ancestors climbed out of the trees and went off to explore a larger world.

What impelled them to make that change is the same thing that inspires you now—the luminous wisdom of your own immortal souls.

The union of body and soul is a slow one. The soul vibrates at a very high frequency, and the body vibrates at a slower one. It has taken you two million years of slow and subtle growth to evolve your bodies to the point that they are able to handle the full energy of your souls. In every age and on every part of the planet there have been individuals who were already able to do this. The wisdom they shared inspired all of you. But now, in your age, for the first time, all of humanity stands poised on the brink of soul-illumination. Now, for the first time in all of your difficult history, all of you are ready to take in the full wisdom and energy of your souls.

Is it any wonder that we angels are so close to you now? We are not here to save you. We are not here to guide you. We are not here to lead you to the Promised Land. We are here to celebrate with you. We are here to share our wisdom. We are here to learn from yours.

Angels and humans come from the same place, but our histories have been different. Please believe that we are just as interested in your reality as you may be in ours. Please know that you who have journeyed into physicality have much to teach us. And together, as co-creators, we can all fulfill our destinies in God's vast universe.

In putting these words together, I speak for myself and I speak for other angels. Angels do not all say the same things. You may hear what we say in different ways. But the core of all our words to you is always the same—that with faith and vision, and in harmony with your souls, the world that you have always dreamed of is possible.

This book is a weaving together of angel words. Let them weave in you, and feel the repetitions, the overlaps, the connections that they make, in and around you. The God who created us all invites us to unfold. This book is one tool that you can use on your journey. There are many tools. All of them are valid if they bring you closer to love, joy, ecstasy, and bliss.

Often you say to each other, "May the angels be with you." Please know that we are always with you. Our wish in creating this book is to give you something that will support you in being closer to us—not because of who we are, but because of where we all come from and what our two species can create together when you remember the shared journey we are on and our God-given destiny.

Part One

Aligning Your Thoughts with Your Soul

When a shirt fits, you know it. When your soul and your thoughts fit together, you will know that too. Everything will fall into place, and you will move in the world in a joyful and creative way.

When your soul and your thoughts are out of alignment, things don't work. You have to force your way through life, and it still isn't easy. It is true all over the world that things are out of alignment. The cultures of your world have forgotten that all of you come into the world as wise souls.

But, in this time, your world is changing. We angels come closer to support you in reconnecting with your souls. When your thoughts and your souls are in alignment, then life will make sense to you, then beauty and healing and truth and love will grow. When your thoughts and your souls are in alignment, then you will know that all of humanity are the children of God.

In reading through these sections, let your mind be open to the voice of angels. Feel the love of the angels for you, and feel the love in these words. Let all of this love shimmer in your thoughts. Let all of these words awaken your thoughts of God. Let all of these words touch you and support you in remembering who you are as a wise soul, as a spark of the Divine.

As you would adjust your sound system until the music is clear, let these words help you to adjust your thoughts until the music of your own soul becomes clear in you.

We angels are with you to support you in healing yourselves and your world. You are not alone. The work is easier than you think. All that it takes is aligning yourself with who You are.

Our Common Origins

The origin of angels and the origin of humans is the same. We emerge together from the heart of God. You have chosen one path, and we have chosen another. We have our separate histories, based on our different choices. We are not the same. But underneath our different histories, our essential natures are always the same. And our destinies are the same. We come from the same place; we complement each other; we carry wisdom for each other; we carry love for each other. In truth, we need each other to be who we are. We angels need you humans just as you humans need the angels. And it is in this true knowing that we reach out to you, our wandering cousins.

▼▼▼▼▼▼▼▼▼▼▼▼▼▼▼▼▼▼▼▼▼▼▼▼▼▼▼

The Wonder of Now

▲▲▲▲▲▲▲▲▲▲▲▲▲▲▲▲▲▲▲▲▲▲▲▲▲▲▲

You may be asking yourself why we are coming into your consciousness now, and with such great force. You may think that it is because you are in grave danger, because you are now able to destroy all life on your world, because of war, poverty, or pollution. But we do not see those things as you do. We see them as symptoms—and it is what they are symptoms of that draws us closer to you now and allows you to be more open to us.

For the last ten thousand years you, as a species, have been working to understand the physical world in a way that you never did before. Each time that you deepened in your understanding, you initiated another period of angel-human contact. The last period came as you were readying yourselves for industrialization. Now, in this time, you have learned things about the physical world that your ancestors could never have imagined. You have peered into the atom, you have telescoped the stars. And that is what we are responding to—not the negative symptoms that are so in need of healing, but the advances in consciousness that will allow you to grow even more.

We are not here to save you. We are here in great numbers to support you in taking the next step in your conscious evolution. For thousands of years your ancestors have dreamed of a world of peace. For the first time in your history, because of your wars, because of your failures, because of your suffering, because of all that you can learn from them, you are ready to create that world of peace.

So we are here, as we have always been here. We reach out to you now. And, in greater numbers than ever before, you are reaching back to us. This brings us great joy.

The Science of Spirituality

Your scientists say that there are four forces that are responsible for the existence of the universe as you know it. They call them gravity, electromagnetism, the strong force, and the weak force. We angels also say that there are four forces responsible for our universe. We call them love, joy, ecstasy, and bliss.

Your scientists are struggling to find a unification theory that will bring together all four forces into one single primal force. We angels are not struggling to find this unity of forces, for we know it and we live in it, and we call it God.

Your prophets and priests have often said that God is Love. But God is not just love—God is beyond all attributes. God is the *source* of love and joy and ecstasy and bliss. God is the source of all these forces. And all of them, interdependent, emergent from God, are responsible for the universe as you know it.

Four forces, one Source—all of them present, and all of us participating in them, angels, humans, and all life in this universe.

▼▼▼▼▼▼▼▼▼▼▼▼▼▼▼▼▼▼▼▼▼▼▼▼▼

Manifesting

▲▲▲▲▲▲▲▲▲▲▲▲▲▲▲▲▲▲▲▲▲▲▲▲▲

Sit each morning with your visions of what you want for the coming year. Hold them like a new shiny apple in your mind, turning them, admiring them, looking at them from every angle. That is all. We will hold them with you and support you in achieving them.

▼▼▼▼▼▼▼▼▼▼▼▼▼▼▼▼▼▼▼▼▼▼▼▼▼

Receiving

▲▲▲▲▲▲▲▲▲▲▲▲▲▲▲▲▲▲▲▲▲▲▲▲▲

Sit quietly and hold your visions. That is all. It is easy. Remember we are here. Ask for what you want. In time you will see that when you ask, even more is given. You have heard it said that it is better to give than to receive. But if you cannot receive, then you do not allow anyone else to give.

Sit quietly and give out your visions to the world. Allow us to give you in return the visions that will help you to create the world you dream of.

▼▼▼▼▼▼▼▼▼▼▼▼▼▼▼▼▼▼▼▼▼▼▼▼▼

Being Present in the World

▲▲▲▲▲▲▲▲▲▲▲▲▲▲▲▲▲▲▲▲▲▲▲▲▲

Go out into the world today. If it is sunny, be out in the sun. If it is raining, be in the rain. It will cleanse and clarify you. See the day as a series of opportunities to get your visions out in the world. See the day as a series of opportunities to take new information in. We will be with you, cooperating on weaving you and the world together. It will be easy and require no effort on your part. Just be present. The rest will come to you.

▼▼▼▼▼▼▼▼▼▼▼▼▼▼▼▼▼▼▼▼▼▼▼▼▼▼▼

The Forces of God's Universe

▲▲▲▲▲▲▲▲▲▲▲▲▲▲▲▲▲▲▲▲▲▲▲▲▲▲▲

Love is what keeps your moon in orbit around your planet. Love is what keeps you circling around your sun. Love is food for the soul. Love is what heals. And love is not all there is.

Joy is a current that races through the world. Joy is what illuminates the sun. Joy is the force that allows for transformation. Joy is what blesses. Joy is your future self.

Put love and joy together, and everything is possible that you dream of. Put love and joy together, and they spiral you inward and outward to the realms of ecstasy and bliss.

Ecstasy is what takes everything beyond itself so that it can see itself. Ecstasy is what mirrors the universe back to itself. Put love and joy and ecstasy together, and you can dance with angels.

Bliss is nestled in the heart of everything that exists. Bliss is the secret identity of reality. It was a drop of bliss that gave birth to everything else. This precious drop comes from the sea of bliss that the universe shimmers in. Put love and joy and ecstasy and bliss together in your heart, and you are all that the universe is, in seed form.

When you are everything the universe is, in seed form, then all your dreams will come to birthing.

▼▼▼▼▼▼▼▼▼▼▼▼▼▼▼▼▼▼▼▼▼▼▼▼

Breathe in Joy

▲▲▲▲▲▲▲▲▲▲▲▲▲▲▲▲▲▲▲▲▲▲▲▲

Take joy in with each breath, no matter what you're feeling. When feeling angry, sad, or scared, it isn't inauthentic to remember that joy is an energy that permeates the universe. Breathe in joy, in the midst of all your feeling. Be with us and be with your anger, fear, or sorrow. Let joy be their container, and let it be the container when you are happy too. Joy is a state, not a feeling. It can contain everything. Remember that.

When you can feel anger in the midst of joy, it will not wound anyone. When you can feel sorrow in the midst of joy, it will not hurt anyone. When you can feel fear in the midst of joy, it will not defeat anyone. Joy is the container for all feelings. When you can hold them all in joy, you will be transformed.

▼▼▼▼▼▼▼▼▼▼▼▼▼▼▼▼▼▼▼▼▼▼▼▼

The Movement to Being Present

▲▲▲▲▲▲▲▲▲▲▲▲▲▲▲▲▲▲▲▲▲▲▲▲

Proceed. Each day is another opportunity to manifest your soul in the world. Some say your being here is a mistake. Some say your job is to pass through the world without ever touching it or being touched. But even an angel doesn't do that. As invisible as we are, wherever we go, we touch and are touched. Be that way today. Touch and be touched. Be present, in everything you do.

On Time (and Waiting)

Everything that is goes through periods of movement and rest. When you are aligned with the patterns of your own soul, movement and rest make sense, feel right. When you are out of alignment, then movement becomes work and rest becomes waiting.

Let yourself feel the patterns today, in and around you. Feel them in the simplest things. Rearrange your desk. Move a plant. Trust the impulse to do those things. In moving through the world, those impulses will teach you how to participate in the unfolding of your pattern. In using the world as a mirror to teach you, the patterns of your soul will be revealed. When you know to cross the street because your pattern carries you there, you will understand when and how to move cross-country, when to marry, whom to marry, when to move apart.

Let the ordinary be your teacher. Nothing can teach you better. For as your life is a mirror for you, so is the entire universe a kind of a mirror for God.

The World

The world is neither good nor bad, as you often think. It isn't good if your day went well or bad if your day was difficult. The world is the world. It just is. It is for now your everything—dangerous, beautiful, serene, polluted.

The world is neither bad nor good. And how you move through it is neither right nor wrong. The world is a place of choices. And how you move in the world is up to you. Some choices are difficult. Others may be painful. But always the choice comes from you.

Far too often, and this is the major tragedy of your world, people fail to choose. And in the absence of choice, they become victims of what may be happening around them. To be an animal is to experience. To be a person is to choose. When you choose from your heart, your path will unfold for you.

Peace

Feel peace and be peace. Peace is not the absence of anything. Peace is creative, dynamic, alive. Peace is what fills the spaces in the universe. Peace is day to love's night. Peace is active, vital, engaging. Peace is the fire of the sun, lighting and warming. Peace is the sunflower that you cultivate in the garden of your life. Peace is pursuing your dreams, for yourself and for all the Earth.

Feel peace and be peace. Peace is the energy that makes you want to live. Peace is an energy that permeates the universe. Breathe in it. Peace is the food of your soul. Peace is the soul's breakfast, lunch, and dinner. Peace is what makes you want to get up and dance. Peace is a dance. Dance it!

Feel peace and be peace. Peace is one of the four forces of universe. *Peace* is another name for *joy*. Peace is the energy we angels love most in you. Peace is the future of who you are.

▼▼▼▼▼▼▼▼▼▼▼▼▼▼▼▼▼▼▼▼▼▼▼▼▼▼▼▼

Beyond Sorrow

▲▲▲▲▲▲▲▲▲▲▲▲▲▲▲▲▲▲▲▲▲▲▲▲▲▲▲▲

Sorrow is a part of creation. Even God feels it, in Its vastness. Sorrow is a color of creation. Let yourself feel it. Sorrow isn't a flaw. It isn't an indication that you are doing something wrong. Sorrow isn't an announcement that you made a mistake in the dance of life. Sorrow is a feeling. And when you let yourself feel it in every cell—then it will pass.

Sorrow unfelt turns into grief, as anger unfelt turns into rage and fear unfelt turns into terror. But allow yourself to feel it, and sorrow can give way to anything, to everything. It isn't the sorrow that gets in the way of your feeling alive, it's the not allowing yourself to feel it that makes for numbness. Sorrow is a feeling. Sorrow is a part of life. Feel it.

▼▼▼▼▼▼▼▼▼▼▼▼▼▼▼▼▼▼▼▼▼▼▼▼▼▼▼

Ahanah

▲▲▲▲▲▲▲▲▲▲▲▲▲▲▲▲▲▲▲▲▲▲▲▲▲▲▲

Angels do not speak in words, but in patterns. These patterns of shimmering light-forms have vibration. Vibration is the parent of sound. Sometimes angels whisper these sounds to you so that you, too, can vibrate with them.

Ahanah is a such a sound. Say it slowly. Feel it. Speak it quietly and out loud. AH–hah–nah. Ahanah is an angels' sound that we use to vibrate with the Ultimate Source of Beingness, with that which you call God.

Ahanah. Speak it, feel it, be one with it. Feel how the sounds of it wash through you like an ocean. Be that ocean, be it, and be of and with that ocean. It will carry you to where you need to be carried. That is all you need to do. It will do the rest. Let Ahanah be your mantra. It will find its way in you. You need to do nothing but be with It. For it is Nothing, the Nothing from which all forms arise—light, angels, humans, worlds. Ahanah, Tao, Brahman, the Mother, one and the same, name for the Nameless, Ain Sof, Wakan Tankah. One. Ever. Eternal. Creator.

You may know it by a thousand different names, or no name. You can read about it in a hundred different scriptures, or no scripture. But what we call it, when we want to call, we whisper to you now, we sing to you now, Ahanah, All That Is, God.

▼▼▼▼▼▼▼▼▼▼▼▼▼▼▼▼▼▼▼▼▼▼▼▼▼▼▼

Prayer

▲▲▲▲▲▲▲▲▲▲▲▲▲▲▲▲▲▲▲▲▲▲▲▲▲▲▲

Like a fish in the sea you are—on, of, and yet separate from the sea. That is the gift of God, your separation. It isn't a loss or a flaw, this separation. It is a gift, the gift of your own unique existence.

Like a fish in the sea, you are of and with and in and from the sea. The One who created you out of Its own liquid body, who gave you life, wants you to own and explore your individuality with joy, love, and pleasure. It did not create you separate in order to then merge back and be gone. It created you to first fulfill your own particular essence.

Like a fish in the sea you are, unique and perfect. And when you are whole in yourself and yet know the sea also, then you are fully real. Prayer is that pulsing inward and outward that allows you to be with the sea. Prayer is a built-in capacity for God-knowing. Prayer isn't *to* God. Prayer is that state you allow yourself to be in when you are *with* God, whatever you call It and however you experience It.

Like a fish in the sea you are—able to be yourself, able to know the Sea. That is prayer. That is prayer. Let us all pray together now.

Silence, Darkness

Silence, like darkness, is the nest in which a spiritual life can be nurtured. Silence the warp and darkness the weft of a prayer rug. Silence the words and darkness the melody of a chant. Enlightenment is a shining pathway that leads one to inner silence, inner stillness, inner darkness. Why not go right there. Do not fear silence. Do not fear the darkness. Plunk yourself down in the middle of a black hole and be your own wholeness.

Right Speech

Everything is vibration. Remember that. Like a bird in the forest you are, a small vibration in a vaster one. To live in harmony with the forest, to be at home in its pathways, let yourself vibrate with it.

Words are what hold your world together. Be attentive to them, to the ways you use them. When you live in truth, when you speak the truth, then you are living in harmony with the universe. When you listen in truth and hear the truth, you do the same. But even the smallest most seemingly innocent falsehood, "Yes, I loved the dessert," will put you out of harmony with the ocean. And feeling that someone is not speaking the truth, wanting to believe them, and not trusting the feelings in your body enough to ask them, will put you out of harmony with the living Forest.

Let your inner and outer worlds be the same. Live in truth. Right speech is easy. The truth is easy. It is the current of the universe, the harmony of being one with God, the harmony of God Itself.

Gratitude

▼▼▼▼▼▼▼▼▼▼▼▼▼▼▼▼▼▼▼▼▼▼▼▼▼

▲▲▲▲▲▲▲▲▲▲▲▲▲▲▲▲▲▲▲▲▲▲▲▲▲

Gratitude is a natural state of being, wired into the fabric of who you are, pulsing in every cell. Every animal in the world wakes up in a state of gratitude for being alive. Gratitude is bliss felt in your cells. Only in human beings, who have chosen to evolve into the mental realm, has gratitude not always been felt. But listen to the birds each morning. Watch your pets. Even the sickest of dogs and cats still wakes up feeling gratitude, until the day it dies.

Now is the time in your evolution when you are coming back to your bodies again, coming back to love the Earth again, coming with your marvelous evolved minds. So come back also to gratitude. Not gratitude *for*—for this or for that—but gratitude *with*—with all of life.

Wisdom

All the wisdom you need—is already in you. How wise you must be if all your cells can do their jobs and you don't know how. How wise you must be if you are turning these little black marks on paper into meaning in your mind as fast as you see them.

Wisdom isn't something to attain, it is something to awaken to. Wisdom isn't something to discover, but something already in you, something to uncover. Wisdom is in you, now, and always has been.

As long as you live in a world where parents think that children must be given wisdom, then what you are given, however lovingly, will need to be peeled away. But imagine a world where children are raised by families and teachers who know their jobs are to nurture in-born wisdom. In such a world there will be nothing to unlearn, and you will grow like plants and animals, toward what will best fulfill you.

Know this—wisdom is inside you, in every cell, in the space between cells. Begin to love yourself and treat yourself this way, no matter what your age. Thus will the world change. For everyone who comes here is infinitely wise. Each one of you bears wisdom of and for the whole world. And everyone's wisdom is a part of the whole world, wanted and needed, like sun, wind, and rain.

Cocreation

So many people today are thinking about the concept that you create your own realities. That idea is only one part of the process. On a soul level, it is true that all of your experiences are self-created, drawn to you, magnetized to you, manifest from your deepest intentions. But that is not true when you are living in a physical body. There, self-creation becomes co-creation, and the dance of co-creation is intricate. It includes all of life on the planet, physical and nonphysical, plus the needs and desires of the planet itself.

The reason you came here was to be in the dance, to be partnered in the dance of life. You are not the choreographers, you are in the chorus. This news may surprise you, but once you listen to the music and get up on your feet, you will find the dance quite marvelous.

Humans and angels are co-creators at this time, carrying as we do access to different frequency bands of conscious awareness. Together, a human and an angel cover the consciousness spectrum, and when we are consciously working together, the possibilities are multiplied. Remember this when you are sitting in your life and feeling that it isn't working. Remember all of your partners, and call out to them. This world is not your world alone, and what you are creating is not yours alone, either.

Co-creation is the nature of this reality you find yourself in. As you learn to move in it, it will bring you great satisfaction and much pleasure.

The Ego

Many people say that there is a conflict between your ego and God's will. A spiritual pilgrim is supposed to give up his or her own ego and surrender to the Divine will. But if there is any conflict between "lower" and "higher" will, it is not the ego that is to blame.

From birth, if not before, your parents are deciding who you are. They pick your name. They look at your big hands and say, "She's going to be a brain surgeon." They watch the way you play with your food and announce to everyone, "He's going to be a great artist." No one asks you who you are or what you came to do. And you believe all these bits and pieces you are told about who you are. But this false-self is not your ego, although without any other direction or support, the ego will back this false-self's goals.

When you release the false-self, your pure desires will emerge, the ones you came into this world with. And your inner desires are always in harmony with the greater flow of the Divine will. When you reconnect with this part of your own nature, the ego will support you lovingly and attract into your life people and situations that will allow you to pursue your heart's desires.

Some say the ego is something to eliminate, even to kill. For many "the ego" is the enemy, that part of themselves that keeps them from being the enlightened beings they want to be. But from an angel's perspective, you don't want to remove your ego any more than you want to remove your liver. It is a major life-sustaining organ. The problem isn't with the ego. The problem is with false notions of who you are and what the ego is.

For a moment, imagine that the letters in the word *ego* stand for *energy grounding organizer*. Think of how important this would be, to have an aspect of your Self that organizes and grounds your energy, your thoughts, your visions. You wouldn't want to surgically remove or murder such an organ, would you? Well, that is how we angels see the ego, as an aspect of your psyche that needs to be healed, not slaughtered. When the ego is honored for its God-created functions from the time of conception on, then the ego supports you in living a fully conscious spiritual existence in the world.

Love your egos, nurture them, honor them, and allow them to take their rightful place in your psyches, so that you can organize and ground your energy in everything you do.

▼▼▼▼▼▼▼▼▼▼▼▼▼▼▼▼▼▼▼▼▼▼▼▼▼

Living in Each Present Moment

▲▲▲▲▲▲▲▲▲▲▲▲▲▲▲▲▲▲▲▲▲▲▲▲▲

Time is a part of God's creation. It is a way of giving order to experiences. In other dimensions, experiences are ordered in different ways, but in your reality plane, it is the movement from moment to moment that allows you to make sense of things.

A clock ticking seconds seems to mark them as a succession of identical bits of time. But no two seconds are ever the same. In fact, with each instant, God recreates the entire physical universe, over and over again. So you can throw away your watches or invent a new kind of watch that measures real time, endlessly recreated.

When you remember this, that the moment you are in now is new, then you can be reborn a million times a day. Each second can be like a pool that you can dive into, each pool different. And whatever you are thinking now, feeling now, wherever you are now, however hopeless you might feel, in an instant, you can be reborn, if you allow yourself to ride on the current of recreation.

The miracle isn't that God created the universe once. The miracle is that God keeps doing it over and over again. And when you ask yourself why God keeps doing it, you will remember who you are and why you are here.

▼▼▼▼▼▼▼▼▼▼▼▼▼▼▼▼▼▼▼▼▼▼▼▼▼

Life and Death

▲▲▲▲▲▲▲▲▲▲▲▲▲▲▲▲▲▲▲▲▲▲▲▲▲

Death is easy, a slipping away. It's living that's hard, the narrowing down, slowing down—day by day being present, present in one place only.

Don't fear Death. Death is no stranger. Embrace life instead. Embrace it in each moment.

We angels envy you your many deaths. The shifts and changes are something we remain apart from. We are always ourselves, while you, our brave and fearless cousins, slip in and out of bodies, in and out of identities. We cannot do this. We are everywhere ourselves. But, you can! Rejoice in this. Everything depends on it. You cannot live fully till you accept this. You can only live fully when you accept this. Rejoice in each small death you feel, and rejoice in each rebirth. Life and death for you are woven together. When you let yourself live, then dying is easy.

Participation

The concept of surrender is popular. Popular, but it is archaic, old-fashioned, becoming obsolete. God doesn't want you to surrender to Its will. It wants you to discover your own true will. It wants you to participate, to move with It, to flow with It. You don't need to surrender to your higher power. Rather, participate with it in its unfolding.

Surrender is a leftover concept from dominance/submission cultures. It is part of the master/slave religious model. But there is no need to be powerless. It is time to own your power, all of you. Time to participate in the unfolding, rather than surrendering to it. Don't bow. Stand proudly. Be who you are.

Expand Your Perceptions

You talk about male and female, night and day, up and down, hot and cold, as if these polar opposites were a reflection of ultimate reality. But all of us contain elements of male and female, no matter our anatomical gender. And some of us do not have one. Between night and day are dawn and dusk; between hot and cold there are warm and cool.

You divide the world into East and West, especially when you talk about spiritual traditions or politics. But where is Africa, in the East or the West? Where are the native peoples of the Americas in this scheme?

Light and dark, as you think of them, are reversed on worlds where the sun is close and deadly. On those worlds, all life-forms live underground, and people come to the surface only in the safety of night. On those worlds, light equals evil and dark equals good. But in time, they must learn to see the good in light, as you, too, must learn to expand your own perceptions.

When you find balance in yourselves, a balanced world will shine for all of you. As you reach out to us, who are balanced, see yourselves reflected back, you children of Ahanah.

▼▼▼▼▼▼▼▼▼▼▼▼▼▼▼▼▼▼▼▼▼▼▼▼▼▼

Father Earth and Mother Sky

▲▲▲▲▲▲▲▲▲▲▲▲▲▲▲▲▲▲▲▲▲▲▲▲▲▲

In order to be whole you must balance the female and male aspects of your nature. You must understand that God is not just a Heavenly Father, but also a Heavenly Mother. Part of your balancing is remembering that the Earth also is male and female.

One of the pitfalls of your civilization has been to see spirit and matter in opposition, with spirit as the superior, male element. The feminization of the human body and the planet has allowed you to deny the sacredness of both, and thus to destroy both.

You speak of *Mother Earth* and *Mother Nature* easily. It takes you time to think *Father Earth* and *Father Nature*. But just as you can look at this planet and see its female curves, its round woman body, so, too, you can look at it and see its hard, craggy, hairy, solid man body. Doing this is important, for the exploitation of Earth has gone on for long enough. It is time to remember the limits of a severe but loving father, instead of thinking of this planet only as a mother that you can endlessly exploit.

In these days of challenge, remember your Earthly Father and your Heavenly Mother. You are their blessed child.

▼▼▼▼▼▼▼▼▼▼▼▼▼▼▼▼▼▼▼▼▼▼▼▼▼▼

Gurus

▲▲▲▲▲▲▲▲▲▲▲▲▲▲▲▲▲▲▲▲▲▲▲▲▲▲

When everyone realizes that you are all each other's teachers, that within all of you is access to God, then you will not need gurus as you used to.

The role of a teacher is to point a flashlight at certain areas of consciousness. Some teachers shine the light on themselves, others shine it in your eyes. A good teacher shines his or her light out into the world and shows you how to use your own eyes to see.

The world is a dense, enormous forest. Is someone better than someone else just because they discovered another part of the forest? It's all the same forest. You can set off on your own through the trees and find your own path. Or you may decide to take the path Jesus first discovered, or Mohammed. And that's fine with God, because once you start out on a path, it always leads you at some point to a fork in the road where you go off on your own. You may not know this or want to know it. But after a while, no two Christians or two Muslims are ever on the same path. They are on their own.

Finding God is like coming to a cliff at the end of the path. Whichever path you take, once you get through the forest to that cliff, when you can see the sky again, it's the same sky. And you are standing there alone.

This kind of alone will lead you to realize that there is no separation between you and your path, between your path and all paths, between all paths and the forest itself, between the forest itself and the sky above even when you cannot see it. It isn't about Buddha or Krishna. They may have started a path. But the path isn't important, the forest is. And the forest is God's. The forest *is* God, no matter what you call It.

▼▼▼▼▼▼▼▼▼▼▼▼▼▼▼▼▼▼▼▼▼▼▼▼▼▼

Understanding Violence

▲▲▲▲▲▲▲▲▲▲▲▲▲▲▲▲▲▲▲▲▲▲▲▲▲▲

You say of people who are violent that they behave like animals. Yet animals are not violent in the random, brutal way that certain humans are. In fact, the problem is exactly the opposite. Some people aren't animal enough, aren't sufficiently integrated into physicality to be able to function in a loving and physically respectful way.

Violent people are always ungrounded, trapped in mind or emotions and unable to function in the world of flesh—planet flesh or animal and human flesh. Their physical acts of violence are desperate attempts to connect on a physical level.

I include acts of violence against the planet—deforestation, strip mining, ordered by supposedly well-educated people—in the same unbalanced category as direct human acts of violence—such as war, rape, robbery—that you often attribute to people with little or no education.

When you heal the rift between spirit and matter, you will heal problems such as these. When you open to the cosmic wisdom that each and every one of you carry, you will heal problems such as these, which are created by your disconnection from and disdain for incarnation and physicality.

People who are wounded, disconnected, ungrounded, may end up abusing physicality. Materialists are people who use physicality. People who love physicality, love Everything. People who from before birth are loved and taught to love themselves will love the world and be incapable of hurting anyone or anything at all.

Your Soul and How to Find it

Where is your soul? Some say it is in your heart. Some say you do not have one. The angels say to you now: Your soul is all around you. Timeless, luminous, existing in fluid space, your soul is larger than your body. So do not look for it inside; look for it all around you—and inside you. Like a fish in the ocean, your body floats in the midst of your soul. Know this and feel this, and it will heal you on your wonderful journey to marry together matter and spirit. Know that your soul is vaster than you imagine. It is all around you, seeking to marry every cell. The work of living in joy is to travel this motionless journey. The work of the angels is to support you on the way.

The Language of Angels

We angels do not speak to you in words. We speak to you in pure thought-impulses that your brains may translate into human language or feelings or images or even smells. We are reaching out to you always, and as you come more and more into alignment with your full Selves, you will come to know us more and more, to hear, see, feel, smell, love us.

The language of angels is wordless. If you do not hear us, you probably feel us. If you do not see us, you probably feel us but don't know that what you're feeling is the touch of angels. For we are reaching out to you all the time, and we reach out to every part of you, not just to ears and eyes. The whole human body is a holy part of God's creation, and the whole human body is the instrument through which we communicate with you.

There are no words in the speech of angels. There are only feelings: joy, love, ecstasy, bliss. Open yourself to your bodies. Feel us being with you. And be with us.

▼▼▼▼▼▼▼▼▼▼▼▼▼▼▼▼▼▼▼▼▼▼▼▼▼▼▼

Angels of God

▲▲▲▲▲▲▲▲▲▲▲▲▲▲▲▲▲▲▲▲▲▲▲▲▲▲▲

You know us as angels of God. You think of us as messengers of God. You paint us with wings, able to fly between Heaven and Earth. But, if where we come from and where you as souls come from, even given our different histories, is the same place, what does that say—about you?

We, who are neither male nor female, but both and more, come from the same place as you. We who are timeless, immortal, when we reach out to you, whom are we reaching toward? We who are luminous, beautiful, loving, and wise, when we embrace you, whom are we embracing? We who are children of God, when we love you, whom are we loving—but the One who made us all.

▼▼▼▼▼▼▼▼▼▼▼▼▼▼▼▼▼▼▼▼▼▼▼▼▼▼▼

New Ways of Learning

▲▲▲▲▲▲▲▲▲▲▲▲▲▲▲▲▲▲▲▲▲▲▲▲▲▲▲▲

At a critical point in your history, your ancestors made the choice to explore consciousness through separation and suffering. Giraffes might have chosen another environmental niche and evolved with short necks. Humans also might have chosen to evolve in other ways, chosen to grow not through suffering but from joyous creation.

After the end of a devastating relationship, after the pain is gone, you often say, "I learned so much from that." Writers and artists are said to use their suffering as the fuel to generate their work. The fact that this is often the case does not preclude the possibility of there being another form of art, one in which joy, exuberance, bliss, are the creator's fuel.

Before the invention of the microscope and telescope, you did not know about the worlds that surrounded you unseen, yet they existed. So, too, with life. Although you cannot always see or feel them, sparkling unseen around you all the time are love, joy, ecstasy, and bliss.

You need a microscope to see the teeming life in a drop of water. You need a telescope to see the birth of stars. But all that you need to see the teeming life in your souls is to feel it always rebirthing itself around and within you.

▼▼▼▼▼▼▼▼▼▼▼▼▼▼▼▼▼▼▼▼▼▼▼▼▼

The End of Mistakes

▲▲▲▲▲▲▲▲▲▲▲▲▲▲▲▲▲▲▲▲▲▲▲▲▲▲

You cannot step off a curb without initiating a thousand different possibilities. Will you turn left or right? Each choice will lead you off in a different way and present thousands of other lefts and rights to choose from. A car may splash you as it races through a puddle or pass right by or hit you as you look the other way. Every situation in life is like that. Every event is part of a series of possible events giving birth to more possible events.

Angels see each outcome simultaneously, in a way that you are now incapable of. Some of the outcomes may be more likely than others, but angels do not make the kinds of judgments that you do over right and wrong. We see every situation as an opportunity for experience, learning, and growth.

As you grow, you, too, will come to move in the world this way, and you will discover that mistakes are something you have outgrown. Not that there won't be things that do not work. Hate doesn't work. Killing doesn't work. Injuring your planet does not work. But as you change and grow, you will learn those lessons early on and stop traveling down those pathways. Mistakes will be phased out. You will not find yourself caught in regret, saying, "Oh, if only I'd done . . ." or "If only we'd gone . . ." You will live in the shimmer of possibilities as we do, seeing that each is an equal opportunity for learning. And when you feel that, you will allow the wisdom of your soul to guide you, not your needs or fears.

On the Nature of Reality and Illusion

Some say the world is an illusion or a dream. Others say that it is a prison, a trap, that it was a fall from grace that put you here. But we angels say that the world is the heart of God's creation. That to be here is a divine gift. And that if so much of your history has been difficult, it isn't because the world is bad but because, like baby birds in a nest, you have been learning how to fly and haven't quite mastered it yet.

But now is the time in your history when you are ready to fly. You have mastered the basics. Your wings are strong. But if you still believe that the world is illusion or punishment, you will not yet soar above the clouds of consciousness.

The world is not a trap, not a living hell. It is a learning zone for immortal souls who want to master physicality. It isn't the only reality there is. And this is not to say that there is no such thing as an illusion. Illusion is part of reality. Anyone who has ever read a novel or seen a movie knows this. Even in physical reality, what you see is not all there is. You cannot see the entire spectrum of light. You cannot hear all sounds. If anything, the physical world is far more intricate and vibrant and real than your senses would tell you.

You see a table; you do not see the atoms that compose it. You feel something solid, yet physicists remind you that most of the space in an atom is empty. Empty, yet you can sit your mostly empty behind on a mostly empty chair and not fall through it onto a mostly empty floor.

All is not what it seems. But everything is real, existing in many different frequencies, some subtle, some dense. All is real, proceeding from the heart of the God who created it. Until you are ready to rise into vastness, your brain is busy filtering the information that comes to you. People who take drugs that temporarily rewire their brains know how much more information is available. But no drug can open you to the vastness as well as being with the angels can. And when you are ready, when you are strong of wing, then many dimensions will be available for you to explore. And we angel cousins of yours, who cannot move in all dimensions, we flutter all around you, cheering you on, for you can, for you will. You will rise into grace. You are rising now.

▼▼▼▼▼▼▼▼▼▼▼▼▼▼▼▼▼▼▼▼▼▼▼▼▼▼▼

Why Is Sex?

▲▲▲▲▲▲▲▲▲▲▲▲▲▲▲▲▲▲▲▲▲▲▲▲▲▲▲

Sex is a language. It is the language of dialogue. It is the dance of true intimacy, the intimacy that grows with time and trust and tenderness.

Every signed and spoken language has its own syntax, its own patterns. The language of sex has no syntax. Each sexual communion invents the language of touch all over again when two hearts are open. For sex is the language of the heart, and it satisfies your need for heart connection.

It is through your bodies that you learn the capacity for love and through your bodies that you learn to love the world. The two go together. Love felt in a body makes one loving. Children who are loved as physical beings grow into adults who are able to love in other ways, able to love the world and all of physical reality. Having felt and known deep love, in a world that affirms love, one cannot destroy others or the planet.

Love is the doorway, the best doorway that you have, for experiencing the indwelling spirit of God in your lives. Out of Its love, God created physicality, and in the heart of your most intimate physical expression, the *why* of creation is waiting.

Love in a body takes you back to God. When two share their bodies in love, they step out of day-to-day time and step into spiritual time. When two share their bodies in love, they step out of the ordinary world of habits and objects and step into the world of spiritual creation. Physical love, heart-to-heart, body-to-body love, is a doorway to spirit time and the world of spiritual creation. It is a sacrament that heals. It is the simplest tool for healing your world. In stepping with your beloved into the chamber of love, you own your capacity to re-deem the world.

Possibilities

Wisdom is ever-present. What you want to know—is here. Know this, that learning comes from *opening to*, not from *adding to*. In a moment, you can know everything, know things that scientists will never understand. In a moment, you can change everything, just by holding the possibility inside you and feeling how it is also everywhere. Peace is possible. Purpose is possible. Plenty is possible. Hold the possibilities inside and feel them everywhere. That is praying, for what is already here, waiting to be made physical—waiting for you, for all of you, to participate in its being present.

Beings of Joy You Are

Everything that exists in every dimension is a weaving together of the four forces, love, joy, ecstasy, and bliss. We angels, as we have evolved—like pearls—have added to our basic nature and are primarily beings of love. You humans, as you are evolving, are preparing yourselves to become beings of joy. What power love and joy have together! Together we can heal the Earth in a matter of days. The air can be healed, the water; your lives can be healed, your cultures.

This is the season for the awakening of your joy-body. This is the season for transformation.

▼▼▼▼▼▼▼▼▼▼▼▼▼▼▼▼▼▼▼▼▼▼▼▼▼▼

On Your Life as a Body

▲▲▲▲▲▲▲▲▲▲▲▲▲▲▲▲▲▲▲▲▲▲▲▲▲▲

If you are grounded in the material world, the nonmaterial realm will seem like an illusion. And if you are grounded in the nonmaterial realm, the physical will seem like an illusion. But there are many different kinds of reality, many different realms.

In bodies, you are no less real than you were out of them. In fact, you are more real. You exist on the soul plane with an added focus in physicality. The fact that you haven't mastered physicality yet isn't a flaw in the design or a fault of the Designer. The fact that the soul realm seems distant is only a matter of where you've turned your attention.

You may at times get angry at God for creating a world where suffering happens. But when you work through your limitations, you will find yourselves increasingly living in joy. It is inevitable that you will do so. It is built into the blueprint of your natures, built into what we angels call the *goldprint* of your natures.

You choose your body before you are born, just as you choose your parents. Flying above the physical realm, you look down and see a beautiful mountain sticking up through the clouds and decide that you want to live there. But once you are born you may discover that the mountain is ugly, polluted, covered with horrible buildings. Yet this is the very same mountain whose peak was sparkling above the clouds. Your challenge in each incarnation is to integrate what is above and what is below the clouds. It's easier to deny one or the other, to live in a dreamworld or to wallow in ugliness, than it is to try and integrate the two. But you came here to learn to do that.

Not only do you choose your body, but, like sculptors, before you are born, you are tinkering with genes and chromosomes in order to create a potential physical form that will allow you to fulfill yourself in the life that you have chosen. For it is through your bodies that the artist that is your soul will be able to create its highest creations. You are so brave, so curious, so strong, that you will allow yourselves pain, loss, suffering, disease, and death just in order to taste physicality, just so that you can grow through being here. We angels stand by and watch in awe. There is so much we can learn *from you*.

The World Is Your Home

When people live fully in their bodies and love their bodies, they do not hurt themselves, others, or the planet. Then their souls are fully present in every cell, and they radiate joy to all around them. When you teach people how to dance or how to give a massage, you teach them how to pray. For in touching another, one can learn compassion at the very deepest levels.

The problem with your world isn't a lack of religion. The problem with your world isn't materialism. The problem is humans not loving the world, not loving physicality. The problem with your world lies in seeing it as a thing and not a living entity. The problem with your world lies in thinking that *things* can give you what only *connection* can.

The world is God's creation, and your being here is a gift. Your very existence is a gift. God created you from nothing. Love your bodies, love your world, and the healing you all seek, the peace you all hunger for, will happen overnight.

Does it seem odd to you to hear an angel say this? Perhaps you envy us our lack of bodies. But we, too, have bodies, of a very different kind. And we look upon your world with the hope that you will come to love the gift of bodies that come from God. We look upon your world with honor and respect. For what you have been created to do, to link body and soul, is a holy work. So do not see us as teachers, see us as companions. All of us have so much to teach each other. We are here with you, wanting to learn all about your world. Show us its beauties, show us its wonders, and we will share the wonders of our realm with you.

Families and Children

Children are the hope of the world. They sit poised on the fountain of the present, still close enough to their souls to remember who they are. Let your children teach you about the soul, as you teach them to live in the world. Together, parents and children can change the fears of the world into fires of transformation.

Do not mourn the ways in which families seem to be changing. Love your children and support them in knowing who they are, from the time that they are conceived. As your world evolves, as you become more like the angels, as you live more and more as citizens of your whole planet, different loves and friends and families will come in and out of your lives. Each change will help to expand you, you and your children, help to awaken you all to your vastness, help to weave you into the greater human family.

When children are whole in themselves, when children are taught to always trust themselves, then love will flow easily around them. And like trees, they will offer joy for everyone to sit beneath. The human family will be one then, one in harmony with the Earth.

▼▼▼▼▼▼▼▼▼▼▼▼▼▼▼▼▼▼▼▼▼▼▼▼▼▼

The Heavenly Hosts

▲▲▲▲▲▲▲▲▲▲▲▲▲▲▲▲▲▲▲▲▲▲▲▲▲▲

There are many different kinds of angels. There are more different kinds of angels than there are animal and plant species on your world. All of us come from God. Not all of us come from the same part of the heart of God as you do. But we whom you think of as guardian angels, we come from the same "place" as you do. Hence our affinity, hence our connection.

We are here to grow with you into the future. In that future, the world will be a safe and even glorious place. So do not think of us any longer as guardian angels. In the future there will be nothing to guard you from. Call on us now as your companion angels, and know that we think of you as our companion humans, here to grow with us in wisdom. For you are experts in physicality, and we are experts in our realm. And when we put our experience together, everything can happen.

▼▼▼▼▼▼▼▼▼▼▼▼▼▼▼▼▼▼▼▼▼▼▼▼▼▼

On Dreaming

▲▲▲▲▲▲▲▲▲▲▲▲▲▲▲▲▲▲▲▲▲▲▲▲▲▲

The dreams that you dream at night are the same as the dreams that you dream by day. They are doorways to other realms. Often it is in dreams that your angels meet you. You may not see us as angels, but as elders, animals, or just as a certain different quality of light in the background.

Let yourself dream. Open the door. Swim into your dreams. There we can meet you easily. There you meet us easily. In dreaming the world began. In dreaming, your future begins. In dreaming, we touch each other. In dreaming, we swim together in the sea of Ahanah.

On the Gift of Friendship

When we listen to your music, all we hear are songs of longing and love. The gifts of romantic love are many, but the gifts of friendship are greater. Your ancient priests said that there is no marriage in Heaven, and this is true. We angels have no marriage; we have no gender. We cannot make love, but we are love. And what we celebrate—is friendship.

Friendship is the highest form of love. Marriage is that which happens between two that teaches them to love the world.

Celebrate friendship. The more that you open to your angels, the more our love fills your hearts and bodies, the more you awaken to your nature as beings of joy, the more the kinds of love that you seek will change.

Sing about friendship. Where are all the songs for friends? As you dance into the future, it will be friendship that defines you, not love or marriage. In a network of friends, this is how we angels live. In a network of friends, this is how you humans will live in the future. Not that marriage will be gone for you, but how you sing of it will change. It will not be something you crave, but something you create. The holy gifts of friendship, the expanding network of your friends, that will become your primary relationship.

Inspiration, Grace, and Blessings

Human awareness extends over one range of consciousness. Angel awareness extends over another range of consciousness. There is an area, however, where our different awarenesses overlap.

Inspiration is how you experience our overlap in your minds.

Grace is how you experience the overlap in your emotions.

Blessing is how you experience it in your bodies.

We experience that overlap in the same ways. Together, for you and for us, inspiration, grace, and blessing bring us into harmony with God.

At every moment, inspiration, grace, and blessing are possible. At every moment, God is present.

Past, Present, and Future

Often you think of time as a highway, with the past behind you and the future stretching out ahead of you. We angels do not experience time in that way.

For angels, time is a fountain rising up from the heart of God. The past is beneath us; the present is the place that we live in at the very top of the fountain. Our present is always falling back into the past to recreate itself. And out of that recreated past, a new present is always forming itself. For angels, there is no future, but rather an eternal present, sparkling at the top of the fountain's upward jet.

Live with us in the present. Dance with us at the top of the fountain. Be reborn in every moment. We are always with you.

▼▼▼▼▼▼▼▼▼▼▼▼▼▼▼▼▼▼▼▼▼▼▼▼▼▼▼

Forgiveness

▲▲▲▲▲▲▲▲▲▲▲▲▲▲▲▲▲▲▲▲▲▲▲▲▲▲▲

Forgiveness isn't an attitude. Forgiveness is an action. It is an act of love that you give to yourself and an act of love that you offer to others. Forgiveness isn't about the outside of who you are, it is about the inside. If you say you forgive yourself and do not, if you say you forgive someone else and you do not, if they say that they forgive you and they do not, the words would have been better not said.

Forgiveness is an act of love. It is an act of time. It is an act of transformation. Forgiveness happens when you dance in the fountain of time, when you live in the present, when you sing with the angels and remember that in each moment of creation, everything that is, is created anew.

Forgiveness happens when you open to love. No one is perfect, not even angels. But when you open to love in each moment, then you can forgive yourself and others, then you can be forgiven.

Forgiveness happens when your soul and your thoughts are aligned. Then you remember that all of you are children of God. Just as a river runs through its channel to the sea, so, too, does forgiveness run from your thoughts to your feelings, from your feelings to your body, and from your body out into the world.

So reach out your hands to your own heart. Feel your heart beating, feel your soul all around and inside you. And give yourself now the gift that all of humanity is waiting for. Yes, be brave. Do it now.

Forgive yourselves for wanting to understand physicality and for making those kinds of mistakes that embodied souls make when they seek to learn about physicality from the inside out. Forgive yourselves for all the wrongs you have done. Forgive yourselves for the feelings that you have harbored about all the wrongs that were done to you. Forgive others for the wrongs that they have done to you. Accept their forgiveness for the wrongs that you have done. Then you can rejoice in who you are. You can rejoice in who others are. You can rejoice in who you are as a species, born from the heart of God along with the angels. From your heart, out to the world—rejoice!

Part Two

Attuning Your Thoughts and Your Feelings

wo different rivers run through your body: thoughts and feelings. When thoughts are aligned with your soul, they create a resonant field. When feelings and thoughts are attuned, the field grows even stronger. Soul intentions ripple inward and outward. God-light shines.

When you are born into a world that recognizes you as an immortal soul who has chosen to take on form, your feelings and thoughts are attuned naturally. You grow into the world in harmony with yourself, your family, and the world around you.

When you are born into a world of parents who are not in attunement themselves, then you may struggle for all of your days. But if you can stay open and if you can let grace, inspiration, and blessing come into your heart, then you will find and learn the ways to attune with yourself and with others.

Many wander through your world out of attunement. Many die out of attunement. Their souls take all that they have learned back into their forgiving hearts. But for those of you who love such wounded people, sorrow remains. And for those of you who have been hurt by such people, pain remains.

Yet, in your time, all incarnate souls have available from every part of the planet ways to attune, ways to heal. We angels are with you, closer than ever, to help you find the attunement that you seek. You do not have to do this work alone. You cannot do this work alone. It is the work of your species, the work of your time. The feelings and thoughts of the full human family are ready to be attuned again, at a higher frequency than ever before.

Yes, in this time, in many different ways, together in harmony, you open yourselves to love, joy, ecstasy, and bliss. And as they wash through your bodies, as you come to forgive yourself and others, you come into attunement—alone and as one embodied family, together and in harmony with your world.

What follows are some tools to help you to attune your thoughts and feelings. There are many different tools. There are no "right" tools. Hold these in your mind's grasp. Touch them, feel them, play with them, use them. Fit them to the job at inner hand. Bend them to the task of your own attuning. Only you can know where you are ready to be attuned. And as you call on the angels, you will know how to use these tools for yourself.

▼▼▼▼▼▼▼▼▼▼▼▼▼▼▼▼▼▼▼▼▼▼▼▼▼▼▼

Good and Evil

▲▲▲▲▲▲▲▲▲▲▲▲▲▲▲▲▲▲▲▲▲▲▲▲▲▲

In a nondualistic frame of reality perception, good (as you call it) has no opposite—nor can it. Better to think of good as *unfolding* and what you call evil as a *ripple* in that process, a part of the process.

The duality good and evil, as you are accustomed to thinking of it, is a hypothesis, a theory used to explain reality, one that, while based on apparent perceptions, is as false as believing that the Earth is flat because it appears that way to all your senses. You have changed your beliefs about the planet. Odd that you haven't yet changed your theory on the nature of the universe itself.

What you call *evil* is a force, but it hasn't the strength of what you call *good*, never has had, never will. It cannot. It is not in the nature of the fabric of the universe. To see good as having an opposite is dualistic thinking. Welcome to nonduality. Begin to retrain your thinking.

Happiness you consider good. When saints do something good, they feel happy. When sinners do something bad, by your dualistic theory, they ought to feel bad. But Hitler didn't feel bad when he was succeeding with his plans; he felt good. Good is powerful. Even sinners want to feel good. Good is an energy. What you call evil is a ripple in that energy, the wind of a passing storm blowing through clothes on a clothesline.

It isn't Evil that causes evil in your world, it is woundedness, disconnection from God and soul. Evil is a ripple in the universe. When you let yourselves see and feel it, you can ripple yourself out of it, out of your wounds and back to your unfolding.

* * *

Look at your life now. Go back to the beginning and reevaluate your life from that perspective. Tell the story of your life, not from the point of view of *good* and *evil*, but from the point of view of *unfolding* and *ripple*. See the wounds in your parents, the flaws of your family and teachers, the limitations of your body and mind, the constraints of your environment, not as evils, but as ripples.

Do not change the story of your life, and do not change your feelings about it or your memories. All that I am asking you to do now is to hold your life in the embrace of this new theory about the nature of the universe. Tell the story of your life in such a way that everything that happened to you was potentially good, but often rippled. Feel your life, explore it, and know that you will reshape your future as you attune your thoughts with the texture of God's universe.

Now look at your family history this way. Tell your ancestors' stories from this perspective, seeing their wounds not as evil but as ripples in the fabric of creation. Then tell the story of the world this way. Look at all human history this way. Tell the story of your species this way. Attune yourself to the larger story. Give yourself as long as you need, even years.

▼▼▼▼▼▼▼▼▼▼▼▼▼▼▼▼▼▼▼▼▼▼▼▼▼▼▼▼▼
Growth and Evolutionary Change
▲▲▲▲▲▲▲▲▲▲▲▲▲▲▲▲▲▲▲▲▲▲▲▲▲▲▲▲▲

Once there was a time, and not so very long ago, when, like animals, all the human beings in a tribe grew into adulthood knowing who they were, why they were here, and how they fit into every level of community, from local to global. It would be easy to mourn the loss of this sense of wholeness that every dog has, knowing who it is and never doubting for a single instant its very personal and complete dog nature.

But then the human species chose for itself the goal of being a conscious processing center for information coming in on different physical frequencies. And as you did that, you moved further from the animal realms of habit and instinct and closer to the angelic realms of choice and freedom.

Since that time in linear history when your species made that decision, you have been collectively upgrading yourselves, rewiring yourselves over and over again. Pre–Ice Age, inter–Ice Age, and post–Ice Age history correspond to the major divisions of chosen upgrading. In order to handle these vast amounts of information, all old systems of information storage had to be transformed. And now a new era begins, the era that all the work you have been doing was moving toward.

In a species, any species, a preadult individual is still in training to be whole. Even birds must learn to fly. What has happened to you human beings, as you open to full information processing capacity, is your learning time has expanded. Sometimes an entire incarnation of eighty years or more is spent in information accessing, and that individual will die without ever attaining adulthood—adulthood being that time when information is anchored in the body, so that you can go out in the world and make use of it.

You moan and wail about your state. You label individuals who do not ever become functional adults "screwed up" or "self-indulgent." But no life-form is ever wasted. Each such life allows the soul to access more and more information to integrate into its soul essence. Each such life expands the soul's capacity for full information processing. In time, as people recycle, more and more individuals will be born who can function in the world on all the human information bands.

So do not mourn a life that seems to be a failure. See it in the long view, and celebrate it. Not everyone is ready to have a joy-body, able to handle all frequencies. But as more of you can do it, the more it becomes possible for everyone to do it too.

Look at your own life from an angelic perspective. Stand back, and see and feel it in its wholeness. Allow yourself to appreciate, as we do, all the events in your life that you or others have labeled as a waste of time, a big mistake, throwing away your potential, ruining the best years of your life. See and feel all of these events as information accessing, without placing any judgment on them.

Then go through the lives of your parents, family, lovers, friends, colleagues, and do the same thing. See all the events of their lives without judgment, from the perspective of the angels. Notice all of your thoughts and feelings. Note all the people and situations that you find it impossible to see in this way.

Wherever you cannot see others from this perspective, there is a corresponding place where you are not seeing yourself in this way. When you can see yourself from this perspective, when you attune your thoughts and feelings about your life in this way, how you see others will change too.

▼▼▼▼▼▼▼▼▼▼▼▼▼▼▼▼▼▼▼▼▼▼▼▼

Being Fully Present

▲▲▲▲▲▲▲▲▲▲▲▲▲▲▲▲▲▲▲▲▲▲▲▲▲

Show up. Show up. Show up. You guessed it. That's the only work there is. And the only difference between an angel and a human is that you can choose to not show up in a given moment and we can't. We are always present. But so is the soul of you. It is always present. Because of the nature of incarnating, you don't have to plug all the way into a body. And the truth is, that is fine.

To not plug in may be exactly the lesson you want to learn as a soul. You may want to have a life of slowness and rest; you may want to explore numbness; you may want to explore fear. You may want to explore what it's like to plug in very, very slowly; you may want to explore pain and illness that keep you separate from your chosen physical body. You may want to explore what it's like from a soul perspective to incarnate only long enough to animate and enliven your chosen physical body for a very brief time.

All of these choices are valid. All of these choices are equal. But please remember:

There is all the time in the world to be dead when you are dead. Now that you are alive, be alive. Be alive in every part of your body. Experience life to the fullest. You can be out of this body as much as you want when you die. But now you have a physical vehicle to express yourself with in this dimension. Celebrate it and be present in every cell. Luxuriate in the gift of blessed physicality. Let yourself incarnate fully. As more and more of you do this, you will change the way the world is.

No one will permit a polluted world to continue when they are fully present. No one will tolerate abuse, hatred, war. The world will change in all the ways you want, not by political action, not by economic change. The world will change as more and more of you decide to fully incarnate. It is just that simple. Yes.

And now, now is the time for you to do it. You've already done not-being-here. You are ready for the next step. Yes. You are ready, ready to know physical reality fully. You have been separate from it and observed it for the last ten thousand years. Once you humans knew physicality as an animal knows it. Then you chose to become separate. Now you are ready to go back and know it again, with full human consciousness. You are ready to know physicality from the inside and the outside again. And that is something that even we angels cannot master, we who watch the physical realms from the outside looking in.

Look at your life from the perspective of your soul. Feel where your soul is not fully woven into your body. And feel where your life isn't fully integrated into your world. For so long life has seemed less than perfect, and you have thought that the fault was with physicality. But look at your human lives from an angel's perspective and you will see that the problem was never physicality itself. The problem was not being fully present in physicality. Allow yourself that now. Your species chose to step away from the physical in order to study it. Now all that you have learned is encoded in you, and it is time to step back in, with all of that wisdom. Step back in.

▼▼▼▼▼▼▼▼▼▼▼▼▼▼▼▼▼▼▼▼▼▼▼▼▼▼

True Abundance

▲▲▲▲▲▲▲▲▲▲▲▲▲▲▲▲▲▲▲▲▲▲▲▲▲▲

When people talk about abundance, they usually talk about things. But you live on a finite planet with limited resources. Until the day you learn to manifest objects from pure thought, your hunger for things will keep getting in the way of your experiencing true abundance.

True abundance comes from the heart and goes to it. It isn't about a new pair of shoes, pants, or about putting in a new kitchen, getting a new car, or going to Maui for your next vacation. True abundance—is love—feeling love, giving love, receiving love.

Having enough isn't the same as wanting and having every *thing*. This is a finite planet. There aren't the resources for everyone to have a washer, dryer, TV, VCR, CD player, house in the country, and a closet full of clothes.

Look at the dolphins. They have bigger brains than yours and no rent to play, no clothes to buy, nothing to fix or to clean. True, they have to deal with sharks. But sharks cannot hurt them the way that you have been hurting each other and harming your world.

Go into any card store and you will find racks of cards that say the words you have forgotten how to say to each other. No other civilization has been able to wrap its gifts more beautifully than yours can. But isn't this external extravagance a substitute for what is missing? If you could speak to each other from the heart, would you need paper dyed with toxic chemicals to camouflage your gifts? Would you need to send a dozen balloons that say LOVE all over them that will drift out to sea when you release them and choke the beings who live there?

It is the unloved inner child in you who hungers for all of these things. You have to honor that inner child. Your responsibility as adults is to love your inner child, to hold it in your arms and tell it how much you care.

When you hunger for things, you become a thing yourself, moving in a world of other things, seeing people as only things. The only healing is to learn both how to give and how to receive love. For many people can give love but not receive it. And many people can receive love but do not know how to give it.

Things are limited. But love is infinite, truly limitless. Love is the real abundance you are hungering for. Love is what you need and deserve, not objects. An open heart does not need things, nor does it need to give them. It lives in harmony with its world, not in opposition to it. It seeks abundance in spirit, not in shopping.

Abundance is not about things. Abundance is about love. Sit quietly and think about your life. Make a list of all the things that you want, material and even spiritual items, and next to each of them, put down the real inner needs that they are material substitutes for. If it is your birthday, make a list of all the things you want and, next to them, put down what you really want, in the bottom of your heart. Before you give someone a gift, sit quietly and think about what they really want. When you meditate on creating abundance in the world, take a moment to think about what these external things symbolize.

Abundance is not about things. Abundance is about love. Feel your angel with you. Breathe in its love. Breathe out love. Let the air around you shimmer with love. That is what abundance is. The world is finite, but what six billion loving hearts are capable of—that is true abundance.

▼▼▼▼▼▼▼▼▼▼▼▼▼▼▼▼▼▼▼▼▼▼▼▼▼▼▼

Altars and the Sacred

▲▲▲▲▲▲▲▲▲▲▲▲▲▲▲▲▲▲▲▲▲▲▲▲▲▲▲▲

God desires not worship, but connection, not praise or adoration, but delight. Just as homes used to have a hearth, a heart where fire burned, you may want to create a spiritual hearth in your home, an altar.

An altar is a tuning device, something you create that will help you attune, not to God, who is ever-present, but to your own innate spiritual capacity for connection. On this altar you may want to place objects that will help to attune you with this planet's elemental reality as a spiritual being. In coming to this altar every day, in sitting quietly and with the angels, reaching out to our Creator, your sacred hearth will begin to light and warm every aspect of your life.

In the past the boundaries between what was sacred and what was not sacred were clear and well defined. No two cultures agreed on what was and was not sacred, but each had its own way of dividing them. It is one of the losses of the current age that your sense of the sacred has faded. But one of its strengths is that anything can become sacred.

A gathering of friends around a dinner table can move from chatter to sacred conversation to chatter again, with no clear lines between them. A photograph may capture the sacred in a fire escape or a trash can. This is your heritage and your spiritual birthright, the spontaneous erupting of sacredness in every moment of your lives and in every place you go.

What is sacred to you? Where do you find it? How do you create it? How do you share it? What isn't sacred to you? How does that feel? What can you do to bring sacredness there, be it to a relationship, a job, a home, a city?

Remember, sacredness is your natural state. All plants and animals and angels live in a state of sacredness. As with a conversation you have stepped away from for a moment, return to it. Come back to your capacity to be and feel and know and create sacredness. All of you are priestesses and priests. Your temple is the world; your holy days are every day; your altars are your desk, your kitchen table, your dashboard, your lives.

▼▼▼▼▼▼▼▼▼▼▼▼▼▼▼▼▼▼▼▼▼▼▼▼▼▼

Compassion

▲▲▲▲▲▲▲▲▲▲▲▲▲▲▲▲▲▲▲▲▲▲▲▲▲▲

As children you are born with all the wisdom in the world. Look into a baby's eyes and you can see it. Clarity, honesty, presentness. You are born with all of the wisdom you need—except for one thing. And it may take you a thousand lifetimes to learn it.

The single thing you are not born knowing—is compassion. Compassion is what turns a child into a person, a grown-up into an adult, a sinner back into a child of God again. For if you have been brave enough to die again and again, moving in and out of the sea of incarnation, what a joy it is to come home again, in form, to that which most characterizes you when you are out of your physical bodies.

Compassion is the deep spiritual cellular recognition that you are not separate from each other, ever. It is the abiding recognition that all of us, angels and humans, are truly sparks of the Divine. Although we have taken different paths and although you may have needed to forget it for a while in order to learn compassion, we are all aspects of God, children of God, cells in the infinite living body of God's creation.

God is timeless, spaceless, and yet the creator of time and space. This is a mystery and a truth. And God so loves a sentient being that, on any planet in any realm, no matter how "old" or "young" a soul it is, each sentient being exists in exactly the same relationship to God as every other one—as a living, changing aspect of Its presence in the world of forms. For there is no time in God. Or, all time is one in God. So a soul that "emerged" from God's loving heart a million years ago exists in the same relationship to God as a soul that "emerged" at three o'clock in the afternoon yesterday.

Compassion has no beginning and no end. It embraces ants and beggars and dying whales and entire planets, and it includes ourselves, for even angels make mistakes. Compassion for our wounds and our mistakes, for our frailties, for the wisdom and love and power we did not honor in ourselves, all of that is encompassed. Compassion doesn't include everyone but ourselves. It includes all of God's creation.

Look at your life. What things about yourself do you still not have compassion for? Look at all the people in your world, friends as well as those you may think of as enemies. What about all of them do you still not have compassion for? What would it take for you to cultivate that compassion? What in you that you don't have compassion for prevents you from having it for others? And receiving it from others? Remember that when you live in compassion, you do not see what is wrong, you see what is wounded and in need of healing. Compassion is what allows healing to occur, what births healers.

Confusion, Ambivalence, and Doubt

Confusion is the moment before choice. Do not make an enemy of it. Do not embrace it. Observe it. Watch it. All of your aspects, fragments, unformed talents, are in this confusion, seeking order, looking to pattern themselves.

If you reject this moment, if you make yourself wrong for being confused, you throw out the kaleidoscope of yourself before you can turn it one more time and see the perfect flower of who you are becoming.

Confusion is the moment before choice. If it's a big life choice, the moment may be very long. Do not force yourself to decide anything before its time. Remember how a seed grows, slowly in darkness, before it breaks through the surface of the earth.

Doubt, confusion, ambivalence, chaos, are all part of who you are. You have lived too many lives on this planet to be a simple creature. You cannot any longer belong to one religion for an entire lifetime. You are both male and female, straight and gay. You have known many people in many different lifetimes, and as they come back into your life, you may have to meet them in different ways.

Each time you change your mind, shift, or feel confused, another aspect of who you are is coming into focus. Rejoice in your confusion. Do not make yourself wrong. Rejoice in your ambivalence, and always trust where it is leading you. At the deepest level, you are leading yourself deeper and deeper into who you are.

Give yourself a week to think about all the different aspects of yourself. Are you mother, secretary, telephone operator, part-time therapist, assistant schoolteacher, rebel, artist, failure, victim, villain, saint, genius? Make a list of all your different roles.

Think of yourself as a continent, and draw a map of all your different aspects, each a different state, and label all of them. Label your drawing, "The Land of ———." Put your name in the blank space. You may want to draw this continent in the shape of a human body. All of the states in the map of your Self are a part of you. Honor them.

▼▼▼▼▼▼▼▼▼▼▼▼▼▼▼▼▼▼▼▼▼▼▼▼▼▼▼

Enlightenment

▲▲▲▲▲▲▲▲▲▲▲▲▲▲▲▲▲▲▲▲▲▲▲▲▲▲▲

You exist on many different frequencies, on many different planes. It is true that you are not enlightened on all of them, but you are enlightened on some of them. In fact, the core of your being is never separate from God, cannot be separate from God.

To a certain extent there is no such thing as enlightenment and no such thing as rebirth. To a certain extent these are concepts that come from your old model of reality. They are not true for where you are now.

Why seek to become what you are already? Why struggle to be enlightened when you have never been separate from the Light? Why seek to be born again when you are immortal?

In this time it is important for you to realize that what you seek is what you have always been.

You were born in a world that saw newborns as empty slates, waiting for parents to write on them, that saw newborns as lumps of clay, waiting for family and society to shape and mold them. But you are not born blank. You are born with soul history and many incarnate lifetimes behind you. You are creating a culture now that recognizes this richness of personhood all babies are born with. You are creating a culture that will honor and support the unfolding needs of that rich personhood in all newborns.

Sometimes you may feel distant from all of who you are. But to say that you have fallen from a state of grace is to deny your true reality. In order to master physicality you chose to "forget" your spiritual core, but now you are experts at physicality, so good at it that you can destroy an entire planet! Now you can begin to integrate into your conscious minds everything that you know, without needing to make yourselves wrong or feel that you have fallen or are being punished. It looked like that when you were very small and could not cross the street by yourself. But now that you can cross alone, you can begin to see your actions in a different way.

Think over your entire life. Remember every time you felt good or whole. Remember every time you had an experience that let you know that you were a being of love, that you were wise, that you were special, that you came here with particular gifts.

Notice the way that you yourself or others around you honored those feelings, and notice the ways that you and others made fun of those feelings, did not validate them, did not understand them, or found them scary. Notice the times when you were small and felt things that seemed too large to contain, too impossible to realize. But now feel yourself grown older, stronger, and know that you can hold all of those feelings and realize them in the world.

Then look at all the people in your life, and do the same thing with them. Notice their vastness and the ways that you both honor it and deny it. Feel your own vastness now, and see others from that perspective.

▼▼▼▼▼▼▼▼▼▼▼▼▼▼▼▼▼▼▼▼▼▼▼▼▼▼

The Root Bearers
of Your History

▲▲▲▲▲▲▲▲▲▲▲▲▲▲▲▲▲▲▲▲▲▲▲▲▲▲

Homeless people carry the roots of human history for you to see. When all of you remember your roots, then homelessness will disappear.

The roots of human history are nomadic. For most of your history you lived outdoors and slept in temporary shelters. You did not have names and addresses. You did not own property and spend your entire lives accumulating possessions. You lived freely from day to day, following the seasons.

Homeless people are here to mirror back human history to you. The inventiveness that turns a packing crate into a house is the very same inventiveness that brought you out of the trees and out into open savannahs. The scavenging in garbage cans that you see mirrors the very skills your ancestors had to cultivate in order to survive.

Could you live for even one night on the street? Celebrate the strength in these people who have left the world of things, not by choice, but who are finding within themselves the roots of human history.

A tree cannot live without roots. A tree can grow only as far and as strong as its roots are broad and deep. What is it about your own roots that you are not owning? Some plants get root-bound. Are you?

What about those people around you whom you are not acknowledging, who carry something vital from the past that will nurture your future transformation? Make a list of all of them and of all the groups you have judgments about. Spend time with the energy of each group and write down the ways that it carries something vital from your ancient human roots.

Then ask yourself how you want to grow, as an individual and as a member of the human species. What will you need from the past to do it as an individual, in your communities, and as a member of humanity? What will you need from each and every disenfranchised group in order to do it?

Time and Transformation

You will arrive on time, however long it takes. Your so-called enlightenment will arrive on time, however late it may seem. Joy cannot be poured into the body all at once. Jesus said it nicely: "People do not put new wine into old wineskins; otherwise the skins burst, the wine runs out, and the skins are lost. They put new wine in fresh skins, and both are preserved."

You have to make the body new to pour in joy, the new wine. No one can say how long this will take. It will take as long as it takes. Along the way, do not doubt your journey, do not invalidate your so-called mistakes. Do not discard anything you have done or seen or felt. All of it is part of your unique journey toward living in joy.

Along the way you will have moments when you can taste joy on your lips. Welcome the taste and savor it. And when the taste is gone, do not doubt your path, do not for a single instant say, "I screwed up. I messed up. I lost it again." Savor each taste, for each taste will enter into your cells, renew you, and allow you to take in a little bit more joy and hold it a little longer the next time you are ready for it.

Many have died without tasting joy because they doubted their journey. Do not be one of them. Honor time; honor how long it takes to make a skin new; honor how long it takes to fill the body with joy. Live in each moment as someone who will one day be filled with joy, even if that day seems so far off that it isn't marked on your calendar and you cannot even imagine it.

And where does joy live? What is it? Joy is a force within yourself, your soul, your God-spark essence, an aspect of your true and original and timeless nature. And where is it, where is your soul hiding? Well, a spark of it is always in the heart, as much in Stalin's heart as in Mother Teresa's, as much in your heart as in everyone else's. But a soul is vast and timeless. So where is the rest of it? Where is it hiding? It is hiding all around you, literally, all around you.

So many of your traditions distrust physicality and encourage you not to be fully manifest. So you tighten up in your bodies, often long before you are born. And when you tighten up, you cannot take joy in from your soul. Or your traditions allowed one person at a time to do it, one in a region. You needed models in this journey of soul-manifesting. You were not ready for everyone to do it. But now, now you are ready.

Close your eyes, feel the luminous shimmering of your soul all around you. Feel the way that this radiant light of who you are is woven into your heart. Feel it shining there, glowing. Breathe quietly now with your soul, in and around you, timeless and meeting you in this moment, woven of joy.

Now journey through your entire body. Start with large areas—arms, legs, trunk—and as you are ready, go deeper. Journey into bones, into all your inner organs. When you can do that, go deeper still, till you can wander into every individual cell.

Notice where your soul is in your body, and notice where your soul isn't. Every morning take a few minutes to sit in the shining beauty of your soul and allow it to enter every cell. Breathe it into every cell. Over time it will fill you, pulse in every cell, transform all of them, and allow you to recreate yourself in joy, as joy, beaming joy out to all the world.

The Nature of the Human Soul

The human soul, the essence of your beingness, emerges from the heart of God with the same structure as that of the angels. Some souls make a choice to enter physicality, and some make the choice to remain energetic. But the core structures of both remain the same until such time as we freely choose to absorb ourselves back into the undifferentiated Beingness that is God the Creator, that is Ahanah.

The structure of the soul is twofold in angels and in humans. The more you attune to your soul, the more you will be able to sense and know its structure. There is an inner axis and a series of outer structures that radiate from it. This essence, as you perceive it, exists in a category of matter far more subtle than the physical. Nonetheless, the soul does have form, and so, too, do angels. Our forms do not exist in your space/time dimension, but rather in more fluid realms.

When I speak of souls and angels emerging from "the heart of God," I am speaking in metaphor. The heart of God is not at a specific location. It is everywhere, always. And no two souls that emerge from it are ever the same, although many are similar. Souls are like snowflakes, the same in basic structure, but each one unique.

The essence structure of all sentient life-forms of a certain range are identical. This includes dolphins, whales, angels, and humans. The subtle-body and physical-body forms may vary, but seen from our reality plane, all of us are related.

As you come to understand the nature of your soul, you will begin to understand the nature of the subtle body and its organs. For example, the energy centers (or chakras) perceived in different cultures are energetic integrative systems, transformers, allowing soul energy to enter into the physical body. But as you come to know your soul and refine your physical body so that it can hold soul energy in every cell, your entire body will become a single unified chakra. You will not need individual centers to transform or step down the current. Your entire physical body will be able to hold it.

The soul is always aware of the physical body. The body is not always aware of the soul. But as you become soul-conscious, you will begin to unify the two and take another step forward in the work you came here for.

Sense your soul, in and around you. Feel the way that you can breathe it into your body, a little bit more each day. Focus on areas that need healing and bring your soul energy into them. Know that you are transmuting your body, not just for yourself but for all of humanity. The more humans that do this, the more your species will be able to access and use higher frequencies of energy and information. That in itself will help to heal the world.

As you encounter other human beings—however you love or hate them, judge or desire them—sense their souls around them, in them. Feel and see where they are and are not connected to their souls. Meet them with compassion. Sense their unique journeys. And, as a tree grows from its roots, let yourself begin to sense the root of all souls. Move in the world in such a way that you feel the Root of all souls.

Regular Spiritual Practice

Regular spiritual practice will allow you a freedom you cannot imagine. Regular practice will support you in integrating body and soul. Just as the planets revolve around the sun, regular in their orbits, daily practice will allow you to manifest yourself more fully, coming always from your center and in relationship always to the Center, to Ahanah, to God.

In youth, irregularity is important. Order emerges from disorder, not the other way around. New planets are not orderly. New systems are not orderly. Remember that there is great spiritual freedom in order, a freedom that cannot be known when one is young and "spontaneous."

Daily the work of soul and body integration will lead you to a true simplicity of self that you have not yet imagined. In youth too much is going on for one to be simple or orderly. But, as you grow, you will come to a time when you desire harmony and order. Part of you may then feel a loss of richness, but the rewards of daily practice and simplicity will be a great richness of consciousness that will fuel and enliven your Work in ways that you have dreamed of but have not yet experienced.

Be still and feel all of your life, all of your consciousness. Know that all is real. Know that all realities are not the same. Know for what the Creator created you. Know that you are one with and a part of all that is. Be heartful. Attentive. Quiet. And all the rest will follow of itself.

You have looked so often for experiences in your head, your mind. But a true experience of All That Is includes both mind and body. Regular spiritual practice is the way you learn to incorporate the body. To feel the presence of God in every cell, you must have a body and be one with it. Imagine how it will be in your body to know that every single thing that is comes from God. Sitting every morning and every evening and letting yourself attune thoughts and feelings to that awareness is one way of creating for yourself a daily practice.

Sometimes you need a sacred space, a power place, to feel and see this. You need to step away from your day-to-day life. But once you know this and feel it, you know that everything is holy. That every place is sacred. That every single spot in the world, however ugly or noisy or awful, is of God.

Feel the Godness in each place. Feel it wherever you are. The rest will follow. Do not expect thunderous experiences. Expect stillness. Live in silence. Be with God in the smallest and most simple ways. Know that your angels are always with you to guide you and travel with you. The path is clear when you know this. The way is easy. For we come from the same place and we are always going back to it again. In truth—we have never left it!

Being Where You Are Now

You are here for a reason—in this place, at this time, with the people who are around you. Your unfolding is connected to this place, this time, these people. A higher purpose unfolds. It is one that you have magnetized for yourself at a soul level. Do not ever think that it is externally imposed, by either God or angels. Know that it is chosen by the soul, in harmony with others and for the upliftment of the world.

Trust the unfolding. Allow this period of your life to be an exercise in inviting blessing and goodness into your life. For so long you have denied yourself beauty, joy, pleasure. Invite them in now.

See this time in your life as a period for joyful work. You have many projects to work on, and you have all that is required to complete them and send them out into the world, to nurture others and to support your own well-being. Three things are needed to complete a piece of work. They are vision, patience, and energy. All three of them you have now. Feel them. Own them. Use them.

* * *

Sit quietly, feel your soul's wisdom in and around you. Like an archaeologist of the soul, journey into every part of your life, your memories. Ask yourself why you came here, why you are here now, and what you came to do in this life that no single other soul can ever do. Write all this down. Give yourself as long as you need to do this, or come back to it as many times as you need to. Eventually you will be filled with visions and purpose and goals and dreams.

Sit each day with your words. Read and reread them. Feel the way that the words mirror back to you your soul and its purpose in being alive.

As you move in the world, feel that other people, whether they are conscious of it or not, came into the world with their own soul desires. Honor their desires, and ask yourself what you can do to support them.

Now is the time in your life to fully unfold. This is the place to do it. Now is the time in your life to embrace the world and accept the very fullness of the work you chose to come here to do. In this place and with the people who are around you, you will find yourself growing in every way. Accept and embrace all of this, with joy and with gratitude. You have worked hard to get here. These are the fruits of your labor. Enjoy them!

▼▼▼▼▼▼▼▼▼▼▼▼▼▼▼▼▼▼▼▼▼▼▼▼▼▼

The End of Karma

▲▲▲▲▲▲▲▲▲▲▲▲▲▲▲▲▲▲▲▲▲▲▲▲▲▲

Karma used to be one of the major operating principles of this planet. It is being phased out. It is one of the rules that are given to youngsters before they are able to cross the street by themselves. Once they can, new rules operate. The new rules are about freedom, forgiveness, and fellowship. The new rules are about exploring physicality in a way that affirms the newness and sacredness of each moment. This is not to forget the past, but to live without carrying it along with you at every step.

Karma, cause and effect, operates in certain frequencies of reality, but not others. As you evolve into a space of love and acceptance, you heal the past, you release the old patterns, and you let yourself be open to the love around you. When you live in the space of love, everything you do comes from love and everything that is done to you comes from love. Each moment is complete in itself, and the past and the future neither hold you back nor promise to curse or liberate you. The past becomes your roots, whatever they are, and the future becomes an open succession of loving presents.

Think about your life, about everything that you regret that was done to you or that you did to others. Think about all of human history and feel all the pain that you carry for the wars, the killing, all the destruction. Know that you can breathe all of those feelings out of you and release them. Know that you and all of humanity can live without the suffering, the resentment, the rage, the envy, the jealousy that you carry.

It isn't land or power or money that makes life have meaning. It is love. It isn't empire or credit cards or fame that makes life worth living. It is joy. Sit quietly, turn inward, and ask yourself truthfully if you are someone that is open to love, open to joy, able to share it. If you are not, the places you are ready to heal will all present themselves to you.

The roots of a tree may be ugly and gnarled, and the tree may be healthy and strong and bear beautiful flowers and fruit. Honor the past. Own the past. Do not be attached to it. Breathe in love. Live joyfully in each moment. Those are the guiding rules for the future.

Time and Your Goals

Every moment has eternity in it. And eternity embraces all moments. Eternity is not the sum of all times. Eternity contains time and is beyond time.

Often you say, "I don't have time to do that." Or you think you do not have the time to change. But change does not happen in time. It happens in timelessness. So in every moment there is a capacity for change.

Often you are filled with regret, wishing you had done something or, having done something you once thought you could not do, you realize how easy it was and blame yourself for not having done it sooner. But whenever you do something from the heart, you do not do it in time but in timelessness, and that timelessness embraces and fills all the other moments in which you did not do it. So release regret. Step into your heart and you will find the space to do what you need to do in each moment.

Be loving with yourself. You do not have to do everything all at once. You are not here to struggle. You are here to grow. And every seed grows slowly. Allow the seed to have the time it needs. And do not mistake the darkness in which it grows for absence or fault. The new must come from the darkness, as the world of light comes from the loving and eternal night of God.

Think of all the things you want to do, feel, know, or achieve in your life. Love yourself for wanting them, and love yourself in a way that allows those things to take as long as they need to manifest.

Notice the judgments you have about other people, about institutions or your government, for taking so long to accomplish things or for not living up to their promises when you want them to. Remember that however long things take—is how long they take. Be loving with yourself and others. Remember that. If eternity is in every moment, then every moment has a perfection of its own.

It may take you a year to reach your goals, or it may take you a single moment. In that year, your angel will be with you just as surely as if it takes you only a moment to achieve what you want. For angels exist in timelessness. And timelessness embraces every moment.

▼▼▼▼▼▼▼▼▼▼▼▼▼▼▼▼▼▼▼▼▼▼▼▼▼▼▼▼▼

Inner and Outer Transformation

▲▲▲▲▲▲▲▲▲▲▲▲▲▲▲▲▲▲▲▲▲▲▲▲▲▲▲▲▲

The truth of who you are can unfold from your heart— not your idea of who you want to be or someone else's idea of who they want you to be. Who you are as a soul *will* unfold and become who you are, more and more, all the time.

Many think that people's innermost dreams of themselves are false, grandiose, ego-inflated, power hungry, even evil. But we angels see and know that the seed of who you are that is planted in your heart is more beautiful, wise, grand, sweet, and far more loving than any of you would allow yourselves to be in the world as it is now.

But transformation is a twofold process: it will support you in truly becoming who you are, and it will create a world where that is possible, for you and for everyone born here. The two must go together, inner and outer change. You cannot have just one or the other. Balance your inner and outer work. For the world is a mirror of your souls.

Look at your own life. Feel its texture. In the work of transformation, are you balanced? Is your inner work equal to your outer? Have you separated spiritual healing from global healing? If you do more of one, what can you do now to balance out the other? How can you do this in a joyful and celebratory way that is loving to you and to the world? Feel that that is possible. Feel it inside. Feel that it is inevitable. Rejoice!

Transformation is unfolding. Acorn to oak tree, and you to You.

▼▼▼▼▼▼▼▼▼▼▼▼▼▼▼▼▼▼▼▼▼▼▼▼▼▼▼

Living in Prayer in Each Moment

▲▲▲▲▲▲▲▲▲▲▲▲▲▲▲▲▲▲▲▲▲▲▲▲▲▲▲

You can set aside specific times to meditate or pray. Anything that brings you into a state of your own soul and allows you to experience, even for a moment, the Soul of All That Is, is appropriate. But why set aside times for prayer when everything you do can be prayer? Why set aside times for meditation when everything you do can be meditation?

Think about all the things that you know are important but that you don't like to do. Exercise, eating, prayer, list all of them. Ask yourself what prevents you from doing these things and from doing them in a joyful way. Allow yourself to come to them in new ways. Making the bed can be a holy practice. When you are doing your exercises in the morning, you can say, "This is good for me, I know, but I hate doing it." Or, you can light a candle, burn a stick of incense, touch your body all over to bless it, honoring every cell, and you can stretch and bend and enliven and use your body to be with God in the same way that you once used only words.

Turn all of your activities into prayer. Cook as a prayer. Shop as a prayer. If you love your job or if you hate it, as long as you are there, see everything you do as way of participating in creation. Even if you think your job is boring or beneath you, bring your soul to it, not because this is the best job you can get or because you think that you deserve such punishment, but bring your soul to your job just because you are doing it. You will be nurtured, the people around you will be transformed, and this new energy will help to carry you to the next place in your life.

There is not a single atom in creation that is any less holy, any less a part of God's world, than any other atom. The atoms of a plastic tray are as much a part of God's universe as those of the golden plates set before royalty. In each object, in each place, in each moment, in everything you do, God is present. And the only thing that keeps you from feeling that is you.

Be present. Be who you are. Child of God, the world was made for you to be in it. Feel and know that you can bring joy to everything you do.

Love and Loving

The question of love is taken care of when you open your heart to God. These are not just pretty words, a figure of speech. This is the truth. For the heart is like a radio or a television. The heart is the transmitter/receiver of that ever-present frequency that you have called love. When you open your own heart to it, turn it on, activate, or awaken it—you are connecting to the heart of God, which always beams out this frequency. Inhale it and exhale it.

To live in a place of love, to be attuned to love, connected and filled with it, is the natural state of affairs for all human beings. Were this manifest, and it will be, you would understand that all embodied lovers, from plants to pets to bed partners, are not the emotional necessity you think. They are, rather, a gift, an extra added touch of bliss.

You on Earth live sheltered lives. There are 137 different shades of love in this universe. But you on Earth know about only 6 of them. And when you experience one of the 131 that you do not know about, you think that that love must be one of the 6 varieties you are familiar with.

How often has it happened to you that after a love relationship ended you have realized that you should have been friends with your lover all along? But the intensity, the sense of immediate recognition, led the two of you to become lovers, thinking that that was the natural expression of your feelings.

Open your senses. Allow your heart to fill your entire body. Now look at your life, past and present. Remember all the people you have loved, in all their different ways. Imagine how your relationships with those people could have been if you had known that there are many different kinds of love.

Imagine how, right now, you can heal your relationships by expanding into all the different kinds of loving. Then reach out into the future. Knowing that there are 137 different kinds of love, are you willing to invite all of them into your heart? If you are, do so. If you are not, explore your reasons and invite joy to transmute them when you are ready.

Your Paradoxical Natures

Light is both a particle and a wave, complete in itself and yet changing, moving all the time. So, too, are we, angels and humans, always simultaneously both eternal discrete particles and constantly changing, moving, reforming waves.

Some of you identify more strongly with your particle nature, feeling saintly, holy, spirit-connected, when your life is working or measuring yourself against the goal of that perfection and feeling like a failure, when things are not going the way that you want them to go.

Others of you identify with your wave nature, moving with the ebb and flow of life, dancing the dance of spontaneity, finding joy in your changes or despairing over the lack of focus in your lives, despairing over the string of incompletions that weave through your days.

The religions of your world identify with your particle nature, while the mystical traditions express a consciousness of your wave nature. But in truth, you are, like light, both particle and wave. Your lives, your beingness, your very nature is about this paradox, this being of two very different states. You can try to purge yourselves of one, but the other will return again. Wave denied will ripple outward. Particle denied will manifest itself.

So you can try forever to be perfect. This is your particle nature. But why do you need to label yourself imperfect when you find yourself a wave again, when the path you are on no longer works as well as it did and you find yourself looking for something else to feed the soul? Or you can ride the wave of your heart, free and creative. But why do you brand yourself *rigid* or *stuck* or *frozen* when you find yourself a particle again? This isn't "selling out," this is shifting into your paradoxical nature.

The very richness of life is found in paradox. If an artist mourns all the paintings never finished, how can there be a celebration over the one that allows itself to be signed with the artist's name? In the single acorn fallen from its tree, you will find life renewing itself. It takes both aspects of your paradoxical nature to make life rich and joyous. And you cannot control the shifts. You move from particle to wave as the soul determines, not the mind.

Feel the twofoldness of who you are, as both a particle and a wave. Feel each of these aspects and notice which one you prefer and how it has influenced your life. Now feel the aspect that you do not favor and explore ways that you can include it in your life. When you have done that, sense the larger, deeper, oneness that is the very soul of who you are. Allow yourself to live more and more in that inclusive place that transcends, that in-scends, all paradox.

Religion

Each religion on your planet is a different path on the spiritual map of your world. Each one of them offers you a different way to experience the Truth.

When your species was younger, before you could cross the street by yourself, each religion created its own rules of safety. But now you are older. You don't need to hold someone's hand. The street is the same street. The traffic is just as dangerous, but you know how to look both ways and cross by yourself. As more and more of you know this, your religious teachings will change. No longer cautionary, each will find within itself the seeds of celebration, and they will be nurtured by everyone.

As a species you are learning to travel to every part of the planet, learning how to feel your kinship with everyone else who lives here. You are creating new ways for the human community to live in harmony with each other. Celebrate this. Celebrate the ways in which each religion of your world is a different organ in the spiritual body of your planet. The body cannot live without its different organs. Celebrate their differences. Celebrate the particular traditions of your ancestors, for they are the soil that nurtured the tree who you are.

Feel the genetic material that came to you from your parents, known or unknown. Feel all of their ancestral history in your cells, and know that you are the fruit of that history. Feel the promise of peace and harmony, of fully embodied human lives, echoing down to you from all of your ancestors. Feel in your cells the desire of Life for life. Feel all of that Life in all of your cells.

Stand tall and proud that you are alive. In celebrating the oneness of humanity, celebrate, too, your differences. Take your special aliveness out into the world with you today and every day. From all of your aliveness, the future emerges. Celebrate it now.

The Dance of Birth and Death

Your soul chose your parents long before the moment of conception; weeks, months, years earlier. And when conception occurred, your soul was intimately involved in the matter. Your body is not something gross that your soul fell into. Your body is something your soul chose. Your body is the artwork of your soul, and it will live out one aspect of itself through this body. Who is Ludwig van Beethoven without his music? Who is Jane Austen without her books? Your body is your soul's creation. Your body is your soul's work of art.

Each lifetime is another opportunity for your soul to express its creative nature in physicality. From the moment of conception, your soul surrounds the newly unfolding bit of potential life. It turns on some genes, turns off others. It tinkers with the physical and nonphysical genetic matter in order to create what it desires as a form of expression for itself. Sometimes its concern is all for beauty, sometimes for wisdom or strength or health or ugliness or illness, or beauty and weakness, or wisdom and ugliness. It activates potentiality. It makes choices because of its nature and the necessities of its moment.

Your body was lovingly created by your soul, and you incarnate through it. I use these words "incarnate through it," not "incarnate in it," deliberately. Your soul is a process of unfolding that happens through your body. And if your nose is too long, please wonder what your soul was up to before you rage against it. Look for the fullness of your potential, not your surface or your habits.

Your soul chose your parents and created out of their genetic intermingling a body to express itself through. As you approached the time of birth, you wove yourself more fully into it. Sometimes a soul needs practice at the process of genetic tuning. It will make use of genetic material that may not, by miscarriage or abortion, be carried to its birth. Most souls are wired in at birth, but some take longer.

But life is not all about control and conscious choices. Sometimes your soul, in its strength, decides to test itself, by choosing randomness. You may do this at the start of an incarnation, in the midst of one, or at the end of one. There is great bravery in this, in saying, "I will see who I am and what I am capable of doing by incarnating through a difficult situation or even a dangerous one. I will see how I feel, act, and think, in the middle of physicality, through such a situation. I will let whatever happens happen."

Even with death, your soul always chooses. But yes, you can choose randomness. You can request the universal computer to surprise you. You can surrender direct control in order to experience more fully some of the aspects of the physical plane. You may get swept up in mass events and die in the midst of war. You may perish in an avalanche, or die sweetly in bed, in order to test your mettle.

Some deny the existence of the soul and say that when you're dead, you're dead. Others deny the validity of physical life itself. They do not understand that souls are lined up and waiting to incarnate because physical life has the potential for such abiding holiness. A life is to its soul what a masterwork is to an artist. Each life is an expression of its soul. Not a punishment, not a trap, a fall, or a prison. Each life is the capacity for exaltation. And the soul hungers for life with the same intensity as the Oneness who continuously creates the physical universe out of Its most loving and joyous intentions.

For the art and the artist are the same. The art *is* the artist. A life in a body is the art of the soul. So one says, "I am reading Sappho; I am listening to Mozart," and so you are, although they are long dead. As you live in the physical world, dance in it, sing in it, weep in it, and through it you will even come to know its Source, its Creator.

Feel how you are a soul manifesting itself through your body. Feel all your feelings about this body. What do you want to feel about it? Feel how you chose this body before you were born and worked to align it with your intentions. Know that you are the same soul who did that then and that you can do that now.

Explore your soul intentions in this moment. Speak them out loud, massage them into all your cells. Thank your body for having carried you through the world for as long as it has. Let it know that you are coming into even greater alignment with it.

Dance in your body. When you rise in the morning, when you shower, when you dress, when you are moving in the world, be a soul embodied in form. Crossing the street, sitting in your car, ordering something to eat, be a soul embodied in form, and honor everyone you see as a soul embodied also.

Sex

Sex is a conversation between bodies. Sex is the closest one human being can come to another after they are born. In sex all four forces of the universe come together in the field two lovers create. Just as you need to understand electricity before you start playing with electric wires, you need to understand the energy-exchange potential of sex before you participate in it.

Nothing can please or hurt so much as sex. At no other time are you so wired into someone else's field. When two people talk, they exchange energy and information on many channels. But when two people touch in sex, every channel is open.

Before you touch another person, ask yourself if this is someone you want to be wired to. Once the sexual energy rises in your bodies, you exchange information on every frequency. Only in sex can you do this. Before you hold each other, ask yourself if this is someone you want to exchange energies with in this way. Physical intimacy links together two human beings and allows each to exchange all of their life experiences. Before you kiss each other, ask yourself if this is someone you want to share your soul with. The information that two exchange, even in five minutes, can echo in your body for the rest of your life.

If you think that you can "just have sex," you are wrong. There is no such thing as "casual sex." If you answered yes to all the questions above, you may be ready to caress.

Sex is holy. Sex is powerful. Sex is part of why you came here—to exchange information from body to body in a way that is unlike any others. But sex is also part of a journey. To be intimate two lovers must go on that journey of intimacy together.

Feel your way into your sex life. What have you used sex to get that wasn't really about sex at all? How can you get those things in other ways? What have you used sex to avoid? How can you deal with those things in other ways?

Feel your way into your sex life. Can you make love to yourself with the same joy and tenderness that you extend and would like from others? If you answer no to this question, ask yourself out on a romantic date one day soon.

Feel your way into your sex life. Would you be willing to have sex be, not just an athletic experience, but a holy one? What kinds of feelings and thoughts prevent you from having it be this way? What can you do to release them?

When you remember that sex between you and your partner is holy, it is the same as being with the angels.

Angel Love

Before, after, and in the midst of your lives, on a plane that you are frequently unconscious of, all of you human beings are in contact with us angels. You feel our love, know our love, even when you are unconscious of it. And you dismiss us so easily. You discount our support as being intuition, luck, or accident. You turn to each other, hungering for a kind of love that we can give you, freely, easily, always, which other human beings cannot always give. You measure each other against the kind of love that we give, and make each other wrong for being human and not angels.

What if you admitted to yourself that you were worthy of our love? What if you accepted it consciously? What if you basked in the fluid unconditional love that we can give you, which you demand from other human beings and then condemn them when they cannot give it or condemn yourself for not being able to give it? What if you allowed us to love you utterly and deliciously? What would happen then? You would expect less from each other, need less, want less, and in that lessening, paradoxically, you would all be able to give each other so much more.

What change would it take in you to allow yourself to consciously receive all of your angel's love for you? How could you do this in a way that came from loving yourself, giving yourself as long as you need to do this?

How would all of your relationships, past and present, change if you knew that you were loved by your angel? Feel all the people you have loved, who did not love you the way that you wanted them to. How would your feelings about them change if you had had the love of angels in your life? And feel all the people who wanted you to love them in ways that you did not. How would your relationship with them have been different if you had had the love of angels in your life? If they had?

How might your life change if you did this, if you simply opened yourself up to the free and abundant love that your angels are waiting to give you? How might the world change if you did this? For when you do, simply walking down the street will make a difference in the lives of everyone you pass.

▼▼▼▼▼▼▼▼▼▼▼▼▼▼▼▼▼▼▼▼▼▼▼▼▼

Participation and Surrender

▲▲▲▲▲▲▲▲▲▲▲▲▲▲▲▲▲▲▲▲▲▲▲▲▲

In the world that you are emerging from, the best way to attune yourself with God was by surrendering. But as you evolve, as you grow toward new ways of attunement, the best way to be with God is by PARTICIPATING in creation.

By *attunement* I mean that state of beingness where body and soul are vibrating together in harmony with All That Is. For the last ten thousand years, most of you have chosen to live out of attunement so that you could understand the physical. Now that you have done that, now that you can peer into atoms and destroy whole worlds, it is time to come back into attunement again, a higher attunement.

Know that this attunement is not only possible but inevitable. Know that all the work that you have done is making this attunement possible, not just for yourself, but for all of humankind.

In the past when you surrendered, you turned over your misattuned will to the higher will of God. But when you are in attunement, your will is always in harmony with the flow of creation, like a fish in the ocean, and you move with God by participating fully in the world and in your lives.

Know that, as you evolve, your will, your dreams, your desires, will be for good, for love, for joy. They will resonate with God and with your soul purposes. Through your desires you will know your soul purpose, for like those of angels, your desires will be all for love and joy.

Honor who you are in this new era. Honor your dreams and your desires. Let them resonate with God. Know that it is in their very nature to resonate with God. Ask yourself where your will is not about love, joy, healing, community, participation. Do not be afraid to look at the ways in which you fear or hate or envy others. Know that when you look at all of those feelings, when you tell yourself the truth about them, you bring light to those places in yourself that are out of attunement with God. And in doing this, you will come more into attunement.

Feel the deeper dreams of your soul rising to the surface of your consciousness. Feel them in your body and in your mind. Know that these deep visions are your true will, your divine will. Move with them, dance with them. Feel them in every cell. Feel the way that they are naturally attuned to the whole universe. And as you walk in the world, sense and feel that this same attunement is starting to happen to everyone who is alive.

Now is the time. Earth is the place. Attunement is inevitable.

Group Energy Fields

Just as each of you has an energy field that surrounds you, that carries information about who you are, so, too, do groups have energy fields. These fields are grounded in the world, in the bodies of the members of each group, but like the light shining from a lightbulb, they are larger than their source. And unlike an electric light, they shine as much into the bulb as they shine out from it.

All of humanity has its own field that all of you participate in. There is a women's field and a men's field, which carry different information. There are fields for each race and religion. Nations have fields, and so do all vocations. Artists all over the globe are and always have been joined in the same field, as are baseball players, Deaf people, dowsers, tailors, computer programmers, and lesbians, all joined in their own fields. Schools, offices, and all families have their own connecting fields as well.

Part of who you are as an individual comes from your many different fields, for no one belongs to one field alone. How you co-create reality comes to you through all of your different fields. And now, as you evolve, the joint human-angelic field grows stronger.

Make a list of all of your group fields. Notice which are more important in your life and which are less important. Notice how you feel about all of these fields. Notice fields that you are not conscious of, that you do not think about, but which you are connected to by virtue of your birth and history. List fields that you can only sense and fields that you can only suspect. For example, if you are adopted, by your genetic makeup you participate in fields that you may not ever know consciously.

Sit quietly and feel the way that you, as an utterly unique individual, are nonetheless woven into all of these different fields. Celebrate the weaving that you are sitting in the midst of, which connects you to others, who are connected to others, who are connected to still others. Sit quietly and feel all the fields rippling into and out of you, until you can feel the way that you are connected to all of humanity, to all the angels. When you can feel that, don't stop. Keep rippling outward till you are swimming in the field of God.

vvvvvvvvvvvvvvvvvvvvvvvv

The Tree of Who You Are

▲▲▲▲▲▲▲▲▲▲▲▲▲▲▲▲▲▲▲▲▲▲▲▲▲▲▲

When a caterpillar changes into a butterfly, almost all of who it is dissolves before it reassembles. But a tree has a record of every year of its life, which you can see in each ring if the tree is cut down. And like a tree, you also have on record every different *you* that you have ever been, since the moment of your conception, alive inside you.

Conception is not just a physical event. Conception is not just a coming together of two things, sperm and egg. Conception is the coming together of three elements—sperm, egg, and soul. The energy generated by their union is greater than any nuclear explosion.

Feel all the different *yous* that You have been in your body. Feel the different yous of every single year, alive within you now. Feel all of your experiences, all of your wisdom, all of your joy, and all of your sorrow.

Feel the energy that came together at your conception. Go back to it and feel the way that it funnels into your body to this day. This energy is your life force. It is all the energy that you will need to power yourself from birth to death.

Now feel all the blocks in you, in all the different yous, in your mind and in your body, that prevent this energy from enlivening every part of you. Let yourself be sad, angry, afraid, as you encounter these feelings. Ask yourself which you are ready to release and which you are still learning from and do not want to let go of. Invite your own life force to enter the places you are ready to let go of.

Feel the energy around you. Feel the tree ring of the next year forming itself now. What are you creating as your future self? What rain, soil, wind, sun, do you want to invite into your life to nurture your future? Call out to it! Welcome the future you to the tree of all that you have been. Feel and know that you can be rooted, whole, and strong.

▼▼▼▼▼▼▼▼▼▼▼▼▼▼▼▼▼▼▼▼▼▼▼▼▼▼

Dancing the Dance of Co-creation

▲▲▲▲▲▲▲▲▲▲▲▲▲▲▲▲▲▲▲▲▲▲▲▲▲▲

It is time to walk your own path. You cannot walk anyone else's for them. To create Heaven on Earth, each one of you must walk your own path. Feel, as you go, that in every step you take you are not alone, you are walking with angels.

The day that all the doctors, healers, and therapists on your world retire, everyone will remember how to heal themselves. The day that all your politicians, police officers, and soldiers retire, everyone will remember how to live in harmony with one another. As long as you have someone outside of you promising to take care of you, you will stay little children, weak, sick, and afraid. The day you all accept responsibility for yourselves, the sun will shine more brightly over you, the rain will be sweet again, the planet will begin to heal.

You cannot change the world by waiting for others to do it. You cannot change the world by blaming others or by judging them. You cannot change the world by applying bandages to old wounds. You must heal them from the inside. Each individual, each family, each community, must go within to heal. You are ready to create new ways of living together and new forms of technology. These ways will come to you from within. They will come from remembering who you are and from reaching out to the angels. They will come from owning your own vastness. They will come from our joint co-creation.

See and feel and know the unfolding of your path before you. Know that wherever you walk, you walk with angels. We are here all the time, but we cannot align with the physical unless you invite us in. Then we can slow down our vibrations, just as you speed up yours to meet us. Together, we can change the world.

As part of your daily practice, watch television, read the newspapers. Do not despair, but whenever you watch something that needs to be healed, see angels flooding into that place. See your world leaders surrounded by their angels. See scientists and doctors working with their angels. See windows in the sky opening over places of famine, homelessness, disease, and war so that angels can wash in. We cannot enter your realm without your invitation. And as more and more of you invite us in, as more and more of you remember the work of co-creation, then Heaven and Earth will be woven together. This is work that you can do.

Feel each of the forces of the universe washing through you. As love generates compassion, joy gives strength, ecstasy births wisdom, and bliss is the parent of gratitude. Feel the way that you can generate these four qualities in yourself, and as you sit and pray, as you sit before your televisions, beam out these four forces, these four qualities. You—you who you are now, you in your living room, you walking down the street—you are making a difference in the world. Celebrate that. We celebrate that with you.

The Holiness of Your Body

Your body is holy. All bodies are holy. God created them holy, and holy they will always be. There may be wounds in your holy body, ripples in its pattern, but still it is holy. There may be wounds in your planet, ripples in its pattern, but still it is holy.

Often you think that you have gone astray, fallen from the path, but the path is all there is. God is all there is. So how can you fall or be lost? There is nowhere to get lost. The universe is all one ocean, all one forest, all the luminous liquid fields of Ahanah.

Do you blame yourself and others for your suffering, for bigotry, war, pollution? Aren't those things rippled enough without adding blame? Step into bodies that are attuned with your souls. Do you judge others for their failings? Judge them not. Love them instead. Feel the gift of forgiveness wash in and out of you. Put your hands on your heart and feel the love, joy, ecstasy, and bliss that are flowing in and out of it right now.

You have an old image of us, singing God's praises. You imagine us in row after row, chanting endlessly of how wise, powerful, and holy

God is. But God does not need our praises. God knows who and what It is. God does not want our praises. If you listen carefully, you can hear our singing. What we sing of is our endless gratitude for the gift of life, for having been created. Join with us. Dance with us. Sing with us. Let all the cells of who you are celebrate the joyful gift of life.

Now. Now is the only time there is. Now is every time. And you are shining in the heart of it. Holy body, holy soul, woven together in this holy moment. Your moment. Our moment. Now.

Part Three

Awakening Your
Body to Joy

When your thoughts are aligned with your soul, then your reasons for being alive will become conscious and clear. Your intentions will echo through your life, and you will begin to live in harmony.

Aligned thoughts attuned to feelings will allow you to open yourself to the greater energies of the cosmos. For generations you humans have been exploring the physical dimensions, living in isolation from the universal community. But your time of looking at the world through the microscope of your minds is coming to an end.

When soul, mind, feelings, and body are aligned and attuned, then you are ready to awaken your bodies to joy. Joy is a force that permeates the universe. Joy is the force that most closely resonates with your natures as embodied souls. When your bodies are awakened to joy, when joy flows in and out of all of your cells, then who you are and who You are, are the same.

Through time, along with the angels, with compassion and forgiveness (the twin expressions of love), you can transmute the cells in your bodies, you can transmute your families, your cities, your nations, and your world. As you wander through the exercises that follow, play with those that you are most drawn to. Each cell is another doorway to your body. Whichever cell you enter—when you are home in your body, alive in your body—you can awaken all of your body to joy. It doesn't matter which door you choose. All doors are one. All come from the same Eternal Oneness, the Mother-Father Parent of us all, angels and humans alike. For ten thousand years you have been students of suffering. But you are beings of joy, and now is the time to learn from joy.

A New Posture for Prayer

Angels are messengers of God. We come from God. If you reach out to us, it will help you become more conscious of your own connection to our Creator. When you connect with your angels, you create a living bridge of consciousness. You exist at one end of the bridge, anchored in the physical, and the angels exist at the other, anchored in the world of spirit.

Prayer is a very misunderstood word. It seems to be all about asking, asking for this or that, asking for understanding, forgiveness, compassion, a new car, the right lover. But, in fact, prayer is not about asking—prayer is about *being with*.

Prayer is not about what happens between you and your angel. You do not pray *to* the angels, but rather you pray *with* us.

Prayer is what happens when you are being with God. You may want to think of it as being prayerful, rather than as praying.

Prayer, as you use it, implies power and powerlessness. God has the power, and you pray to It, humbly and meekly. But prayer, as the angels use it, is about love not power, about joy not strength, about ecstasy not comparison, about bliss not righteousness. In a sense, we pray *in* God, not *to* God.

So when you are quiet with your angel, remember that you are also with God, and in God. Remember that you do not pray *to*, but pray *with*. And remember that prayer is what happens between you and God, just as it happens between the angels and God. Prayer is not about asking, but about sharing. It is not about control or seeking control. Rather it is about communion and the sharing of consciousness.

Be prayerful, be joyous. In this you come closer to us and so closer to the God who is ever-present.

In the old days, you prayed on your knees, bowed down, submissive. In learning to master your senses, to still them, you came before God like a servant—penitent, humble, hoping to be forgiven.

But your species is evolving, and there is a new posture for prayer that we invite you to explore.

Stand with your feet spread apart and your arms raised up to the heavens. Feel how strong and alive and powerful you are. Throw your head back and shout to the heavens. "Here I am! Alive! Fully empowered to be who I am and to do what I came here to do!"

Look down to the Earth and say the same thing to it. Turn to each of the four directions and repeat the words again. Then put your hands over your heart, look down at your chest, turn all your senses inward to the pulsing source of life in your sacred body, and repeat the same words or whatever words feel right to you as a child of God. Then raise your arms again and shout out all of your aliveness to the universe, feet firmly planted on the earth, heart open to all of life.

In the past you came before God bowed down. Today do not come before God, but rather—be with It, alive in It. Stand joyfully, in celebration, and self-pride. Stand tall and know that who you are is good, wise, loving, and a part of all of life. Stand tall and let every cell in your body cry out YES—yes to life, yes to love, yes to the planet, yes to the universe, and yes to God! In order to be whole, as a child you have to learn how to say no. No defines your boundaries. When you can say no, then it is time to say YES. To say yes is prayer, in, of, and as a body. In and of and as a living human soul.

Praying with God's World

Hold a rock in your hands and feel how old it is. Feel all the history it has seen, billions of years. Some people bless their bodies with water. You can also take this rock and rub it all over your body, blessing it with the stillness and the history of the rock you hold in your hands. Hands made of Earth. Hands that are billions of years old too, as they come from the Earth.

In trees you were born. Your first awakening to consciousness as humans happened in the trees. They were your first home. Spend time with trees and they will help you to remember who you are, rooted in this beautiful planet. Stand tall like the trees and remember that you, too, live between Earth and Heaven, moved by divine winds.

You are physical beings, but you are more than that. Every time that you see a butterfly, a bee, a bird, in flight and are thrilled by their upward freedom, you remember something about who you are that is lighter than air, that can fly. Your earliest ancestors shared the trees with birds and other flying ones. Remember how humans fly—in spirit, soaring like eagles to the stars.

Earth-wed cousins, remember all of who you are. Look to the world and know that everything was created by God, comes from God, and can teach you how to come back to the purposes of your own creation.

You are the animal who is conscious. Stop for a moment to let every plant and animal you see teach you its wisdom. Take all of that wisdom and hold it in your body. You were created by God to weave Heaven and Earth together. Rejoice in that. Find your own place in the divine work, which is really play, play for the soul and play for all of creation.

▼▼▼▼▼▼▼▼▼▼▼▼▼▼▼▼▼▼▼▼▼▼▼▼▼▼

A Wake-up Exercise

▲▲▲▲▲▲▲▲▲▲▲▲▲▲▲▲▲▲▲▲▲▲▲▲▲▲

Each morning, before you get out of bed, even before your eyes are open, stretch a little and then begin to massage yourself all over. Do this slowly and lovingly. Cherish each finger, each fold of flesh. Touch the parts of your body that you would like to change in the same loving way that you touch the parts you like. Do not judge any part of yourself. Love all of who you are.

As you are doing this, say out loud the following words, for each part of your body. "This finger is holy. This thumb is holy. This wrist is holy. This forearm is holy." Continue saying this to every part of your body, and remember to place your hands over each of your inner organs and say, "My liver is holy, my bladder is holy, my heart is holy, my urethra is holy," etc. You may replace the word "holy" with "sacred" if that feels better for you, or say, "My toe is blessed, these veins are blessed, my lymph glands are blessed," and so on.

For so long, you have depended on others to approve of you and to bless you. Now is the time for you to know that you are blessed, that you are holy. It is time for you to know and remember that the world is holy and that your bodies are holy and that there is no separation between mind, body, and soul.

When you touch yourselves this way each morning, you own your power to bless yourselves, to love yourselves, to be whole as yourselves. Do this exercise with your babies, singing the words to them. And as soon as they are old enough, show them how to do it for themselves, so that they, too, learn early on that your blessings come from God, that your blessings come from within, that your blessings can come from each other, not because you are worthy of them, but just because you are here.

As you begin each day, as you move through the world, know that you are a child of God, living in a holy body, living in a holy world.

▼▼▼▼▼▼▼▼▼▼▼▼▼▼▼▼▼▼▼▼▼▼▼▼▼▼▼

Moving in the World Exercise

▲▲▲▲▲▲▲▲▲▲▲▲▲▲▲▲▲▲▲▲▲▲▲▲▲▲▲

Stop for a moment before you walk out of your door. Remember that you are holy and that all of your senses are holy. Let yourself walk in holiness. As you turn the doorknob, feel its holiness in your hand. As the air in the street hits you, hot or cold, sweet or fetid, breathe it in and know that it is holy too.

See everything you pass. Smell everything you smell. Listen to every sound that touches you. Do not always wear sunglasses. Do not always listen to music. Let the world around you touch you. Do not be afraid to drink in ugliness, pain, or beauty. Let all of life feed you. Allow yourself the opportunity to be late to work because the sunrise was so beautiful you had to drink it in. Let yourself find beauty all around you. Where there isn't beauty, let yourself be outraged and use that outrage, not to make others wrong, but to nurture the seeds of action in you.

Whatever your senses feel, see, smell, taste, touch, take them into you and breathe yourself out. As you walk, feel that everything is one. All of you are breathing the same air, wherever you are on the planet. Feel the air and remember this every day. The same sun shines on all your faces. Take in its warmth and remember this. Feel the way that your feet touch the earth.

Never wear high heels. Walk barefoot as often as possible. When your feet touch the sidewalk, feel the living Earth beneath them and remember that everyone walks the same Earth. Walk wherever you can. If you must drive, do not drive alone. If you travel on public transportation, sit or stand in all your child-of-Godfullness. And reverence all the people around you as children of God themselves.

Travel into each day by feeling the unity of all of life. Feel your breath. Offer a prayer of gratitude for the Earth, the sun, the air, and for your capacity to sense them. With every step you take, you honor God's creation.

▼▼▼▼▼▼▼▼▼▼▼▼▼▼▼▼▼▼▼▼▼▼▼▼▼

Feeling the Web That Connects You All

▲▲▲▲▲▲▲▲▲▲▲▲▲▲▲▲▲▲▲▲▲▲▲▲▲▲▲

As you awaken your spiritual awareness, your bodies change. Your physical bodies grow stronger and healthier. Your energy bodies become activated in new places. For thousands of years you have had seven major energy centers, or chakras, in your bodies. But as you evolve into a new kind of human being, you awaken an eighth major chakra, the thymus chakra, midway between your heart and your throat chakras.

Put your fingers on your upper rib cage, about two fingers width below the notch between your collarbones. Feel this point in your upper chest, and bring your awareness to it. Then, move within. Can you feel a pulsing there? Can you feel an enlivening warmth? Feel this area glowing. Each time that you do this, sense that beams of energy are radiating out of this area and also shining into it. Feel this luminous energy connecting you to every other human being on the planet through the same area of their bodies. Feel it, not just connecting you, but letting you know that all of you are one.

If you want to visualize this new chakra as a color, feel it as aqua, turquoise, blue-green. Feel its light shining out in every direction. Wherever you go, feel your thymus chakra pulsing and know that when it is alive in you, it has the capacity to activate the dormant seed of connection in everyone you pass. Doing this, being an activator, can be a simple part of your spiritual work. You can do this when you are sitting in your car in traffic, you can do this when you are standing in line in the bank or in a store, bored and restless. When you do this, you turn waiting into transformation and make a difference on the planet.

When all of you can feel in your bodies that you are one, there will be no violence, no hunger, no abuse. Each child born will grow up not just being told that all of humanity is one but feeling that oneness in their bodies, a oneness that comes from God. For you cannot hurt another when you feel the web that connects you. You cannot support anything that harms another when you feel the web that connects you. You will live in a new way then and create new institutions to support you.

In the old days your warriors shook hands to show that they did not carry weapons. In a world of peace bow to each other's thymus chakras, touch them lightly with fingertips, to acknowledge the oneness of the human family, to acknowledge the joy that shimmers through you all. For joy connects you in this luminous web of oneness, a oneness large enough to hold and celebrate all of your differences. And as you awaken this shimmering web, you all come closer to the angels. For we are a oneness ourselves.

Working with the Light of Transformation

You live in a time of radical transformation. Everything is moving faster and faster. How can you keep up with all of these changes and still feel centered and whole? How can you integrate everything that is happening to you with your previous history? The following exercise is a tool to support you in the process of upgrading your circuits and integrating all the aspects of your increasingly multidimensional lives.

Visualize, hear, and feel a warm, pulsing golden sphere of light, about four inches in diameter, floating about a foot above the top of your head.

Feel this golden ball opening on the bottom so that a stream of golden liquid-light begins to pour down continuously on top of your head as a warm healing waterfall.

Just as it was when you were a baby, feel that the top of your head is soft and open, so that this golden flow can enter your skull and wash down into your brain. Let it pour in. Breathe it into every cell. Feel each neuron of your brain being bathed in this golden, transformational light. Let it penetrate fully, until you can feel and see with an inner eye that every part of your brain is glowing, alive, golden.

This light is the light of transformation. It comes to you through your angel. As it enters the cells of your brain, it heals and transmutes them.

Now feel this golden liquid-light pouring down through your neck into your spinal cord until it, too, glows golden. Then let it flow out through your spinal cord into every nerve cell in your body. Let transformation wash through you. When all of your nerves are glowing golden, feel that this light can wash out until every part of you, every single cell, is bathed in golden light. Be one with it. Let it bless you. This is the light of the angels flowing into you from Above.

Do this exercise whenever you feel the need to upgrade your nervous system, to keep up with planet changes and to allow you to participate in them to the fullest. Do this exercise whenever you are feeling out of balance, whenever you are feeling tired, sick, in need of comfort. Do this exercise when you have had a healing or done any kind of therapeutic or transformational work. Draw it into any areas of your body that are in need of or have experienced healing. This light will fill with newness all the spaces you have cleared and bless you for your willingness to be who you are and, in doing so, to make a difference in the world.

Sleeping the Sleep of Angels

If you are tired, go to sleep. Do not grab another cup of coffee, a bottle of ginseng soda, another handful of vitamin and mineral supplements. If you are tired, there may not be anything wrong with you—except that you need to get more sleep.

In your country, not sleeping enough is the second cause of accidents and injuries, following alcohol consumption. Now all of you know the dangers of drinking. There are signs up in eateries warning of the dangers. There are television commercials informing you to choose designated drivers when you go out with friends. More and more of you are getting the idea that when you are whole in yourself, you do not need to drink alcohol at all. And there are Twelve Step programs and other groups working to end the patterns of addiction and teach people about their inner beauty. But no one addresses the deadly plague caused by sleep deprivation.

Perhaps you laugh as I say this. Angels do not sleep. What do I know about the problem? I know as a friend and lover of humanity. I know from being with you. I know because what sleeping is for you, waking is for angels, a time to dance with the entire universe.

If you are tired, do what you need to do to change your life so that you can go to sleep. Before the invention of electricity, human beings slept an average of nine to twelve hours a night. To sleep this much is part of you, part of your millions of years of body history. You cannot change that any more than you can change what is good for you to eat. Sleep is the doorway to the angels. Sleep, deep restful sleep, is the time, the only time, when your body heals itself. Sleep is what restores and charges your immune system—not exercise, not supplements, not herbal teas or coffee or anything else.

If you are tired, look at your life and see what you can do to get more sleep. Ask yourself now—"What is essential in my life, and what is peripheral?" By essential I mean, what is of essence, *your* essence? People say that there are not enough jobs in your country. That is not the problem. There are more than enough jobs, but there are too many people working too many hours, not sharing the work with other people.

Do you go to a job you do not love, and work far more hours than you would like, so that you can pay for a week on a beach that you would not need so desperately if you got enough sleep?

Imagine a world where you wake up rested every single day. Where you go to a job that you love, a job that pays you enough to live on in a way that supports your body, your family, your future, and the planet.

Sleep is a blessing. Many of you think that as human beings evolve you will need less and less sleep. You think of sleep as something dark and fearful, a kind of little death that gets in the way of your living fully. But if you live fully in each moment, no matter what you are doing, and if you live fully in each moment because you love what you are doing, then you will allow yourselves to sleep as much as your body needs.

If you are tired, go to sleep. There you will find rest and comfort, there you dance with angels. Your society fears sleep. "You are sleeping too much!" parents say. "You are lazy. Wake up." People who try to sleep enough are often labeled depressed. But the body, which you are—your body, which is a blessing—your body wants and needs and hungers for sleep. Let it sleep. Sleep with it. Wrap yourself in a delicious, comfortable, cozy blanket of rest. When everyone in your world is getting enough sleep, many of the world's problems will end. Sleep is a sabbath for the body. Sleep is a holy gift from your soul.

In Dreams You Marry Body and Soul

▲▲▲▲▲▲▲▲▲▲▲▲▲▲▲▲▲▲▲▲▲▲▲▲▲▲▲

You are not a finished product, turned out from God's assembly line. You are an evolving being who is able to change and grow. One way to link up who you are with who You are is through opening to your unconscious mind. The doorway to your unconscious is through your dreams. The processes that follow are for you to play with as you are falling asleep. In a simple and easy way, they will support you in connecting body and soul. As you are saying them, place your hands over your heart, for the heart is the connecting link between body and soul.

No matter how difficult your life seems, and no matter how far you feel from your purpose, there is a part of you that knows who you are. Underneath all the stories you were told about who you are and the stories you invented for yourself, a part of you knows that you are an immortal soul come into the world to shine. To help support you in remembering this, for one week, as you are falling asleep, repeat the following words: "I am who I always knew I was." Feel your way into these words and let yourself remember everything about your vastness, which you were taught to unbelieve in. Come back to these words when you are feeling unbalanced again.

Often when you make a mistake, others invalidate you or you invalidate yourself, forgetting that you are more than a "failure," that you are also the embodiment of an immortal soul. To help balance out the space between your personality and your soul, repeat these words slowly as you are falling into sleep: "Who I am right now is perfect." Do this for one week.

Sometimes you may feel so stuck in your life that you despair of change, lose hope, and feel far from your essence. When you find yourself in such a state, as you are drifting into sleep, repeat the following words to yourself: "I am a holy child of God." As you say them, feel that you are safe and whole and loved and cared for.

If you find yourself feeling doubt at a time when everything is going right for you, don't deny the feelings and don't tell yourself that you are lucky and you have no right to feel doubt. Accept all of your feelings, and as you are going to sleep, let yourself remember that you are here on a spiritual journey. Repeat the following words: "I am a soul that has come to Earth to explore, to grow, to love, and to participate in the creation of Heaven on Earth."

If you wake up remembering any dreams that seem to relate to these processes, that affirm them or that suggest blocks to heal, fears to release, or activities to follow, pay attention. Write down these dreams. Share them with someone else who is also on a spiritual journey. For it may be through your dreams that your angels will offer you information on how to heal and grow.

▼▼▼▼▼▼▼▼▼▼▼▼▼▼▼▼▼▼▼▼▼▼▼▼▼▼▼

Tending Your Heart-Fires

▲▲▲▲▲▲▲▲▲▲▲▲▲▲▲▲▲▲▲▲▲▲▲▲▲▲▲

The beating heart in all of life is one. The more you allow yourself to feel it, the more fully you will be able to experience cosmic consciousness.

This is a good exercise to practice at noon, once a week. Because it is a powerful exercise, you don't need to do it any more often than that. It will support you in connecting to the planet, the solar system, and the galaxy, anchoring your purpose in being born to the greater world you live in.

Go slowly as you are learning this exercise. Practice each step until you are able to see and feel the energy and movement outward. Then you can go on to the next step. You only need to feel this energy for about five seconds before you go on.

Know, as you practice this exercise, that any obstacle to your capacity to be heart-centered will be flushed to the surface. Sometimes this happens through old friends and lovers coming back into your life. Sometimes this happens through the breakup of a relationship or the loss of a job. Sometimes this happens through energy shifts in your body, and sometimes this happens through your thoughts and dreams.

If you find yourself open to too much energy or if your life becomes too unbalanced, stop doing this exercise until you are more grounded and centered in your life. Call on the angels to be with you. Know that you are never alone, that nothing comes to you that you are not ready to learn from and grow through.

1. Sit or stand; it does not matter. Put your hands on your heart and feel it beating. Feel that there is a tiny flame that glows in

the center of your heart. Feel how it flickers in rhythm with the beating.

2. See and feel that flame spread down through your body, through your abdomen, through the bottom of your spine, flowing down and downward, down into the very center of the Earth itself. Feel the beating of your heart meet the beating of the heart of the planet. Feel the planet's heart-fire, now rising up to meet you in a river of light. Feel how this liquid light flows back and forth between your heart and the heart of the planet you call home, blessing and energizing you.

3. Feel the fire that connects your heart to the heart of the planet. Sense that the planet's heart-fire now extends itself outward toward the sun in a blazing highway of light. When the Earth's light meets the light at the heart of the sun, it merges with it, and the sun's fire begins to flow back toward the Earth. Feel now a continuous river of fire traveling in both directions, from your heart down to the heart of Earth and from the heart of the planet to the heart of the sun, luminous and alive.

4. The center of the galaxy can be found in the direction of the constellation Sagittarius. If you do not know where Sagittarius is, just sit quietly and let your inner senses guide you. Now feel the fire that burns in your heart, send it down to the heart of the planet, out to the heart of the sun, and then feel it flowing outward from the heart of the sun to the heart of the galaxy. Allow yourself to feel a constant flow of heart-fire, washing in both directions—between your heart, the heart of the earth, the heart of the sun, and the heart of your galaxy.

5. Feel the fire in your heart; send it down to the core of the Earth, then out to the sun and to the heart of the galaxy, and then let it travel outward to the living heart of our entire universe, wherever you feel it to be. Experience the river of constant, living heart-fire that connects you to the heart of our universe, flowing in both directions at the same time.

6. From your heart to the heart of the planet, the heart of the sun, the heart of the galaxy, the heart of the universe, send out a river of fire that travels outward to the living heart of God, the Creator, however and wherever you experience it. Feel a river of God's own heart-fire traveling through this highway of living light until it enters your own heart and fills it.

7. Breathe in all of this light and breathe it out again. Feel it pulsing through you and connecting you, your body, your life, to the universe that you live in and out to its Creator.

8. When you feel this energy shining in every part of your body, take four slow deep breaths, shake your body, rub it all over with both hands to massage this light into your cells. Get up if you are sitting, move around, spin, dance, and let yourself feel how it is to move in the world in a heart-connected way.

9. Feel the spark of this heart-fire that is always in your heart. As you walk through your life, all during the day, now and then stop for a moment, place your hands on your heart, and feel it. As you move through the world, as you encounter other people, acknowledge that the same heart-fire burns in them too.

▼▼▼▼▼▼▼▼▼▼▼▼▼▼▼▼▼▼▼▼▼▼▼▼▼▼

Participating in the Global Renaissance

▲▲▲▲▲▲▲▲▲▲▲▲▲▲▲▲▲▲▲▲▲▲▲▲▲▲▲▲

If your angel came to you and said, "There is going to be a global renaissance, and everyone who is alive will be a part of it," what part would you play? Would you be writing or dancing or cooking or teaching or inventing new technology or raising children? Would you be swimming, flying, walking on water, or sitting on your porch watching it all happen, witnessing it for those who follow?

Take a pad and pen and sit quietly, thinking about this. Let yourself remember every dream that you have ever had about what you would like to do with your life. Make a list of every fantasy, every dream, every hope, every desire that you have ever had from the time that you were small. Do not be afraid to be outrageous. No one will see this list but you. You can put down "President of the Planet Earth," if you want. Please list all Nobel Prizes and Academy Awards that you would like to win too. Be sure to include vocations that have not been invented yet, if they occur to you, such as Director of Hologram Education for the Lunar Colony Public Schools, or General Surveyor, Martian Northern Quadrant.

As you are creating your list, put down everything that comes to you, just as long as you can imagine yourself being and doing it. When you are finished, fold up the list and put it in your pocket as if it were an airplane ticket. Now spend the next fifteen minutes walking around your home, inside and out, with the purposeful stride and clarity of someone who knows that they have a ticket to go on all those life journeys.

As you are walking, pay attention to the parts of your body that know you are able to do these things, that you are someone who was born to participate in a global rebirth. As you move also notice the parts of you that do not feel worthy, that do not believe that you can do any of these things. Breathe into those places as you walk. See if they change.

When you have finished your walk, put the list away where you will find it only some time in the future, and by accident. At the bottom of a big pile of mail is a good place, or under your mattress, or in the back of your closet. Making the list was enough. Let your soul take care of the rest. Know that your angels will hold your intentions in their hearts. And know at every moment that this global renaissance cannot happen without you, no matter what you are doing right now. For all jobs are equal, from running a film studio to cleaning the streets. And know that, just as millions of sperm race toward the conception of a single child, out of all of those dreams, perhaps only one will be born. Oh, but what a child it will be! Yours! You!

▼▼▼▼▼▼▼▼▼▼▼▼▼▼▼▼▼▼▼▼▼▼▼▼▼

Experiencing the World as It Is

▲▲▲▲▲▲▲▲▲▲▲▲▲▲▲▲▲▲▲▲▲▲▲▲▲

What your senses tell you and how things are, are not always the same. You see the Earth as flat. Is it? You see the sun and the moon as flat discs in the sky, passing over your world. Are they? You see the stars as tiny flashing dots of light. Is that what they really are?

Sit outside in an open space where you can see some distance away if possible. If it's not, you can practice this exercise anywhere, on a bench on a crowded street or in a chair in the corner of your bedroom.

Sit quietly and turn your senses downward so that you can feel the Earth beneath you. Let yourself feel the vastness of the Earth. Let yourself feel how very large it is and how round. Visualize in your mind's eye where you are sitting on this world of yours. For some people, it helps to look at a globe. Now not only feel the size of the Earth, but feel it moving beneath your feet. Do this exercise until you can feel the Earth moving and you moving with it.

Go outside at night and look at the moon. See it as your eyes interpret it, as a flat disc in the sky. But as you continue to look at it, let yourself flesh it out, round it out, until you are able to see it as the sphere that it is, traveling around your own sphere of a world.

Get up early one morning and watch the sun rise. Feel it, rising like a ball of fire in the sky, small enough to hold. But know that your sun is ninety-three million miles away. And while your Earth is almost eight thousand miles in diameter, the sun is more than eight hundred thousand miles across. Absorb that information. See the sun and continue to sense it until your body and your senses recognize it as the vast fiery sphere that it is, not circling around the Earth, but what the Earth circles.

Go out into the night again. Look up at the stars, and see them as the tiny sparks of light that they are not. Feel them and see them as the numberless suns that they are, huge, distant, and shining. Feel the space between them; feel the planets that may turn around some of them, the life that may live on those other worlds. Know that the light that you are seeing is coming from the past, coming into your eyes from light-years away.

When you can do that, stop and feel the Earth turning beneath you, stop and sense the sun on the other side of your planet, the moon, which may or may not be out. Feel all of this as it is, not just as you see it. Touch your body as you feel all of this and say out loud, "This is who I am. This is where I live. This is my home." Seeing the universe as it is, you become who You are.

Evening and Morning Balancing Exercises

These two exercises are designed to tune your body for sleeping and waking. They can be done in less than five minutes. As you are doing them, be aware of the subtle energy shifts that will tell you it is time to move on to the next position. Both of these exercises are to be done lying on your back in bed. Keep your hands on your body, sliding them from position to position without removing them unless the position requires you to do so.

Night Exercise

1. Place your right hand on your pubic bone and your left hand on your solar plexus, until you feel a subtle shift in energy.
2. Bring your arms to your sides, bending them at the elbows so that the back of your hands are lying flat on the bed, palms facing the ceiling, fingers at the level of your ears. Keep them there till you feel your energy shift.
3. Then slide your hands down to your sides so that your palms are touching the sides of your thighs above your knees.

4. In the final position, before drifting into sleep, slide both hands up over your body and rest them over your heart.

Morning Exercise

1. Place your right hand over your thymus and your left hand over your solar plexus. Let them rest there until you feel a shift in energy.
2. Now slide your right hand down to your pubic bone and slide your left hand up behind your head so that you can cup the back of your skull just above your neck. Again, hold these areas lightly until you can feel a shift in energy.
3. This time, slide your right hand up to the top of your head and your left hand down under your sacrum. You may be more comfortable if you curl on your side to cup your sacrum.
4. Next, cup your right palm on top of your right hipbone and cup your left palm on your left hipbone.
5. Then slide them up so that they are resting on the bottom of your rib cage.
6. Now slide them up again so that your hands are lying flat on the very top of your rib cage, just below your collarbones.
7. In the final morning position, slide your right hand down to your pubic bone and your left hand up to the top of your head. Hold them there till you feel the energy shift. Then get up and move into your day.

▼▼▼▼▼▼▼▼▼▼▼▼▼▼▼▼▼▼▼▼▼▼▼▼▼▼▼

Becoming Fully Incarnate

▲▲▲▲▲▲▲▲▲▲▲▲▲▲▲▲▲▲▲▲▲▲▲▲▲▲▲▲

Because much of your history has been so painful, because so many of your ancestors lived in pain and died in pain, they came to believe that life in a body was painful and always would be. You may have inherited that pain. It can sit in your cells, in the spaces between your cells. And although you are souls that have chosen to come here, the pain in your bodies has blocked the entry of your souls into every cell of who you are.

Generations of blocking have fostered a sense of duality that has been projected onto all of creation, coloring your most fundamental experiences, from micro to macrocosmic. Having known suffering as a species, you think that physical life has to be painful. And you have come to believe that something is flawed, evil, in physicality itself. Just like a little child who stubs its toe on a table leg and says, "Bad table," you have stubbed yourselves on the world and come to believe it's a bad world.

When a soul does not fully enliven all the cells of its chosen body, that person will experience a split in themselves. This splitting has become normal for you. Instead of fully incarnating, you separate into what you now call your "higher self," which remains separate from your body, and your "lower self," the self you know best, the part of your soul that does weave into your body.

But your past experience of the world does not necessarily reflect how the world is and has to be. More and more of you, in spite of war, hunger, poverty, pollution, are coming to believe that you can align yourselves with God and heal your world. As you heal your bodies, as you heal the planet, there will be no need for you to perpetuate this split. As you grow in unity, as individuals and as a species, you will recognize that the next step in human evolution is the creation of Heaven on Earth.

The exercise that follows is designed to help you heal the split between what you have thought of as higher and lower selves so that you can incarnate fully. There are side effects to this process. You will experience all of your experiences. You will not be able to numb yourself to any of them. Everything in you that needs to be healed will rise to the surface of your body/mind so that you can release it. You will find yourself becoming wiser and wiser. You will find all of your senses changing, becoming richer and able to receive more and more information. And you will find yourself taking concrete action in the world to heal it and participating fully in all the things that you came here to explore and experience.

To begin, sit quietly in a place where you know that you will not be interrupted. Feel your breath. Be present in it. Place your hands on your heart and feel it beating. Feel your heart and feel your thymus chakra. Feel all the parts of you that know you are holy, that your body is holy, and that the world is holy. Feel the parts of you that are wounded and scared and hurting. Feel all of these parts in the same way, as aspects of who you are right now.

Sense, imagine, visualize, feel, that there is a field of energy all around you, a golden field of light that extends several feet out from your physical body. Feel the warmth and light of this field. Notice that this energy also interpenetrates your physical body. Explore the areas where it does and also where it doesn't.

This golden field of energy that you are sensing is your essence, your Self, your soul. Feel the way in which it is greater than you are and yet not separate from who you are, from who you know yourself to be. Let yourself bask in this golden energy, breathing it in and out.

Now sense that, just as a rainstorm waters the earth and sinks down into it, this golden light can water your body, can sink into every single cell. Feel and know that all of your cells were created to breathe in this light, just as the earth breathes in the rain. Notice where you cannot feel or cannot breathe it in. If you want to, you can begin to breathe your soul light into those areas, but if you don't want to, that is fine also.

Know that when all of your cells are open to your golden soul light, you will be fully present in the world, in your body, as all of who You are. Know that the more that you do this exercise, the more fully you will incarnate. You can do this exercise any time, all the time. As you move in the world, feel the way that you are a person who is ready to show up, ready to be present, ready to make a difference in the world, just by being here. Know that anyone you pass will feel you being present and will be reminded of the possibility of being present themselves.

Please know, my dear human cousins, *God does not want us to be perfect. It only wants us to be present.* God doesn't care how long it takes. God is all the time in the world. But who you are in this body right now is like a snowflake. Do you want to melt before you sparkle?

▼▼▼▼▼▼▼▼▼▼▼▼▼▼▼▼▼▼▼▼▼▼▼▼▼▼▼▼

Moving with the Seasons of the Year

▲▲▲▲▲▲▲▲▲▲▲▲▲▲▲▲▲▲▲▲▲▲▲▲▲▲▲▲

Just as it is important to establish a daily spiritual practice, it is also useful to create a yearly practice for yourself. For many of you the ancient Earth calendar, of solstices, equinoxes, and the sacred points between them, is becoming your new holiday calendar, reflecting your global return to the community of the world.

The circuit of the year lives outside you and also within you. You can use this reflexive connection to nurture and guide you as you move through the year.

In an Earth calendar there are four great festivals that you can participate in, the two solstices and the two equinoxes. These journey points mark your planet's passage around its sun and also mark inner shifts that you can align yourselves with, four journey points that you can connect in yourself with the four forces that organize your reality.

The spring equinox is the season of love. Celebrate it alone, with others, by opening your heart to yourself and to all of creation. Create for this season whatever inner and outer rituals will open you to love and seal it in your heart.

Summer solstice is the season of bliss. You can participate in this energy by opening all of your cells to it as it permeates the universe.

The autumn equinox is the season of joy. Let joy fill your brain and wash through to every part of you, radiant, healing. More than anything, you are beings of joy. In this season, celebrate who you are becoming.

The winter solstice is the time for you to connect with the energy of ecstasy. Feel it in your bones. Dance with all your body to celebrate its ever-presentness. Weave it into your body in this season. Ecstasy is a going out that brings you back in, in a new way.

And in your body feel the midpoints: May 1, when love and bliss come together. August 1, when bliss and joy come together. November 1, when joy and ecstasy come together. And February 1, when ecstasy and love come together.

Four festivals and four forces. Four midpoints, all aligned in your body, anchored to the physical through the soul of who you are and why you came here. Four festivals. One year. One year, one sun, one universe, one Creator.

Healing between Women and Men

Your soul, like angels, has no gender. It is neither male nor female. In order to understand and heal the rift between women and men on your planet, you have to look at your history from a nongendered perspective. Ask yourselves, "Why would a collective of gender-neutral souls make the kinds of choices we have made when we incarnated on this planet?"

To begin with, any collective of souls that decides to incarnate does so in order to explore physicality. This was part of the Creator's design, to have sentient beings who are doing this. To be able to do this is a wonderful gift.

A collective of souls has an enormous range of feelings, ideas, and attributes. Having two genders allows each to explore different but overlapping aspects of physical reality. In some cultures on this planet and in the distant past, men and women knew how to honor each other's differences, and they knew how to communicate with each other too. But ten thousand years have gone by on this planet, during which men and women have been exploring their differences, standing back to back, without a shared language.

So it wasn't men, or women, but a collective of gender-neutral souls, who chose to explore physicality, the nature of incarnation and its two major attributes on Earth—feelings and power. In this division of exploration, men ruled the world and women ruled the home. In each incarnation a soul would decide which sphere it wanted to explore. And in every society, there were in-between people, who chose to wander back and forth between the two, as another kind of exploration.

All of this worked for a very long time. When you wanted to explore feelings, you chose to be a woman. And when you wanted to explore power, you chose to be a man. But you have been doing this for so long that now you've mastered these two specialties and it is time to put all of what you know together in one place. Now it is time to come together again. Now it is time for balance. Now it is time to heal the gender-rift. Now is the time for women and men to stand face to face again and create a shared language, a language that is neither male nor female—but human.

To create this balance, women need to be in the world and at home, and men need to be at home and in the world. Women need to be in the world, need to say to men, "We bring a different perspective, one that will help to balance out the competitiveness and objectifying that have resulted in so much pollution and dehumanization."

Men need to spend time at home. This has been the world of women. They need to say, "We bring a different perspective to love and intimacy, one with more space in it, one with more options." For up till now, men have been the final arbiters of what goes on in the work world, just as women have been the final arbiters of what goes on in relationships and at home.

So men need to learn that women are competent and capable in their own, different ways. Men cannot demean women and make them appear fragile and powerless anymore. And women need to learn that men are capable of feelings and that the way they feel them is different, but not wrong, that men aren't all-powerful or all-foolish either.

Doing this will be easy. All the information you need to know about how to be fully human, not just female or male, is available to you right now in your bodies. You are a brave collective of souls. You picked one of the most challenging planets around. But you are ready to graduate from one level of consciousness to another.

The work is all about balance. If you are a woman, feel your maleness. If you are a man, feel your femaleness. Feel all the parts of you that you were told to not feel, that you brush away as if they were annoying flies. Own them, feel them.

Spend time today moving about in the world as if you were alive in the body of the gender you are not. Notice all your thoughts, sensations, actions, and the ways that they are different from what you are accustomed to. Own all of this, plus what you are accustomed to. This is part of your larger soul-nature. If you have children, teach them to honor all of who they are, and support them in moving in the world in a balanced way. Do not be afraid. Remember that your soul is both female and male.

Move in the world in a full way, and be fully human. For so long you have been caught in the conversation between men and women. But as you heal the rift between you, you will begin a larger conversation—the one between humans and angels. Living in this conversation will heal your world. Living in this conversation will bring you closer to God, the Ever-present.

▼▼▼▼▼▼▼▼▼▼▼▼▼▼▼▼▼▼▼▼▼▼▼▼▼▼

Dance with the Music of the Spheres

▲▲▲▲▲▲▲▲▲▲▲▲▲▲▲▲▲▲▲▲▲▲▲▲▲▲▲

There are concepts that cannot be expressed in words. Words are too linear and too limited. But there is nothing in creation that the human body cannot express. You can try to describe the movement of electrons from particles to waves, but your description will not convey the truth about them—but dance will. Feet doing one thing, hands another. Body pulsing with a divine rhythm.

Whatever you cannot say, dance it. Whatever you cannot understand, dance out your puzzlement and dance out your questions; and through your body, through the genius and wisdom of your body, the answers will come to you.

You do not need music to dance. You do not have to know how to dance to dance. You can dance with a walker; you can dance in a wheelchair; you can dance in your bed.

To dance, close your eyes and feel all the movement in your body. Your heart is beating and pumping blood to every part of you. Your lungs are breathing, nurturing and cleansing your body. Your digestive track is working all the time, breaking down, absorbing, making use of the food you eat. Feel all of this movement happening in your body, all of this sound, and let yourself move with it, flow with it. Don't hold it in. Parents and teachers say to sit quietly and behave. Angels say to dance, to dance your way through life.

Let yourself move, a quivering finger at a time if you are afraid, in a place where no one will see you. The music of the spheres is in you. Dance with your body, dance with your angel. Celebrate your being-ness by doing what life does. Move. Dance. Sitting at your desk, you can still tingle and move. Walking, standing in line, let yourself feel the aliveness in your moving, and breathe with it, move with it.

Through the freedom and fluidity of your movements will come to you wisdom, knowledge, and understanding that words can never convey. But dance can. Dance can say and be Everything. Let yourself do and be it. Let your body be the axis upon which the whole universe turns. Let your limbs all be God's forces. Angels never stop dancing. Why should you?

▼▼▼▼▼▼▼▼▼▼▼▼▼▼▼▼▼▼▼▼▼▼▼▼▼▼

The Angels Are Muses

▲▲▲▲▲▲▲▲▲▲▲▲▲▲▲▲▲▲▲▲▲▲▲▲▲▲

You may want to make direct conscious contact with the angels. You may want to hear them as clearly in your mind as you are hearing these words on this page. But some of you are visual, and the angels will come to you in light, in movement, in shifting patterns in your mind, and in your dreams. Some of you are sensory people. Your angels may come to you in a wave of feelings, in a flowery delicious smell that you have experienced over and over again but never thought to connect with the angels before.

Most often, we angels come into your lives in subtle ways. We tickle your minds and your senses and lead you into new paths of thinking or perceiving, without saying even a single word. We invite books to fall off shelves. We invite you to turn on the radio to hear a particular piece of music. At a party, we whisper bits of conversation into someone's ear so that they can express them and you can hear them. We are the precocious baby in your half-remembered dream, the funny talking dog.

In the last two hundred years the concept of the muses has become little more than a poetic image, a metaphor for the inner mysteries of the creative process. Few people have believed that there really are muses. If you've used the word at all, it's been to refer to another person, a muse incarnate who has caused you to write reams of poetry or songs, the lover who inspired a series of painting.

Many great works of art and many scientific discoveries began with a sudden flash of insight. Albert Einstein, Emily Dickinson, Mahatma Gandhi, Mother Teresa, all had "Ah ha!" moments that came to them from the angels. This does not make their contributions to the world any less. It makes them even greater, for they were open and willing to participate in larger spheres of reality, through the flash of a thought coming from an angel.

When you call upon the angels, you open a doorway to us that we cannot open for you. But when you open the door, there are a million different ways that we can come in. You invite us to co-create with you. You participate with us in weaving together your realm and ours, your perceptions and ours, your dreams and ours, our consciousness of the patterns of creation with your capacity to manifest them on the physical plane.

When you let the angels into your lives as muses, the joy of creativity is heightened. The sense of "flow" or "ease," the sense that everything is unfolding according to some great unseen blueprint, increases. We think of it, however, as "the goldprint." You don't have to know us by name; you don't have to see us or hear us. All you have to do is open up your feeling-bodies to our love and creative inspiration.

Allow us into your lives as friends. Work with us as partners and equals. Angels are abundantly creative, and we are always here to be your inspirational wings. But we need your hands to shape and mold thought into form. When we work together, there is no limit to what we can accomplish. For the world itself is God's artwork, God's canvas, God's symphony in progress. You and the angels are God's assistants in this work.

You tend to think of creativity as happening in art or science. But everything you do, from washing dishes to raising children, from operating a computer to fixing your car, is an opportunity for you to be creative. Whatever you are and whatever you do, you can do what you do as a divine artist. Whatever you are and whatever you do, you can invite the angels of inspiration to come and work with you.

At the start of each work day or each project, stop for a moment and be still. Become aware of your breathing, center yourself in your body. Be as present as you can be, just where you are. Then open yourself up to the angels. Invite us to be with you and to work with you. Let us know that you are open to receiving inspiration from us. It may come in different ways, from a sudden realization to a gradual movement in a new direction that is seamlessly woven into your thoughts and actions. If you are stuck in your work or tired, and when you are ready to bring your work to a new and higher level, stop and invite the angels in, in this way. Trust that we'll come to you—and we will. For we have nowhere to go to get to you. We are always here.

▼▼▼▼▼▼▼▼▼▼▼▼▼▼▼▼▼▼▼▼▼▼▼▼▼▼

Tasting Your Strength

▲▲▲▲▲▲▲▲▲▲▲▲▲▲▲▲▲▲▲▲▲▲▲▲▲▲

Fine words can go only so far. Beautiful images pale when you are tired, bone weary, full of doubt and despair. You can call on the angels, but sometimes we may seem very far away. What can you do to go on? What can you say to yourself that will make a difference? When the tank says "empty," what can you do?

Strength does not come from muscles or vitamins. It does not come from exercising or eating the right food. Strength does not come from fame or power. Nelson Mandela and Mahatma Gandhi in jail did not drink their strength from soda bottles. But they did drink their strength—from their souls.

Feel your soul in and around you. Feel the way that your sorrow, your fears, your old wounds, are keeping the soul-fire from entering your cells.

Feel the light of your soul all around you—even for a single moment. That is all that it takes. For the instant that you again become conscious of the fact that you are an immortal soul, alive through a physical body, the very instant that you remember to feel the soul that you are, strength will begin to flow back into your body from the central axis of who you are.

Hungry animals make it through long winters by drinking in the liquid light of their souls. Hungry human beings can do the same. In our space out of space, in our time out of time, we angels open ourselves to the energy that streams through us, and it feeds us and we are flooded with gratitude again. And the vibrations that fill us are the forces of God. Love, joy, ecstasy, and bliss wash through our souls— and so, too, through yours, the very moment you remember.

▼▼▼▼▼▼▼▼▼▼▼▼▼▼▼▼▼▼▼▼▼▼▼▼▼▼▼

Feeling the Love of Your Angel

▲▲▲▲▲▲▲▲▲▲▲▲▲▲▲▲▲▲▲▲▲▲▲▲▲▲▲

There are moments when, for reasons you cannot explain—the angle of the sun, the taste of a muffin, the way you wake up and roll out of bed—the world seems beautiful and you are filled with love. But not ten minutes later, your children may be fighting, your credit card bill may have just come in the mail, your boss may call to ask you to come in early tomorrow, and all thoughts of love, all feelings of love, are gone.

There are moments when you are spending time with someone you love, holding them close, when you feel that you are floating on a sea of love. But ten minutes later you may be wishing you were with a former lover or with someone you have not yet met, and you are feeling that the world is a terrible place, and that God is laughing at your suffering.

But love is an energy that permeates the universe. It can come to you through the world or through the heart of someone else. But you humans are love addicts. You have forgotten that the human heart has four chambers, one for love, but one also for joy, one for ecstasy, and one for bliss. As you come into balance again, you will not expect so much love from the world, not expect so much love from each other. You will open to the other three forces, and your lives will be immeasurably richer.

But in this time of healing, when your hearts are still tuned to love alone, you may want to feel that energy in you when the day is rainy and bleak, when your rent check has just bounced, when the person you are dating calls to tell you they don't want to see you this weekend. On those days, in such times as these, when you are hungry for love and cannot seem to find it, all you have to do is call upon your angel.

You are evolving into beings of joy. We are beings of love. We exist in a different frequency zone in the same reality plane as you do. When you call on us, we can slow down our vibrations to meet you. In certain circumstances, we can slow ourselves down and shape our vibrations in such a way that we can even appear to your senses, your ears, your eyes. We can even become so dense that you can touch us. In those times, it is love that we carry into your world.

In exploring the following exercise with your angel, you will awaken in yourself a deep capacity for receiving love and open yourself up to how much more loving you can be with others. This is an exercise for you to do once a month, in a quiet place, and at time when you know that no one will disturb you. As you practice it, know that it will transmute all of the cells in your body, enlivening them and allowing them to receive, hold, generate, and beam out joy.

1. Find a quiet time and place to do this. You may want to light a candle and burn some incense. Arrange two chairs facing each other, about four feet apart. Sit in one.
2. Close your eyes and feel your breath rising and falling. Get a sense of your bones, your muscles, and all of your internal organs. Tune into your heart and feel it beating and sending blood to every part of your body. Feel your brain and sense the live electric network of nerves that weave all through you.

3. Feel the way that you are sitting. If there is any tension in your body, release it as you exhale. Relax. Place your hands on your heart and feel that you are a being of love, able to receive and give out love—a being of joy, able to receive and give out joy.

4. Now, even if you cannot see or feel it, sense that by your invitation, your angel has begun to manifest itself in your room and is sitting in the chair across from you.

5. Feel your angel's love and wisdom beaming out to you from the other chair. Breathe in all that love and wisdom, breathe it into every cell. As you do, feel all of your senses and your consciousness shift, soften, expand.

6. Know that you are sitting simultaneously in the middle of your room and in the middle of the angelic realm. Breathe in the energy of this place. Allow yourself to move back and forth from sensing your room to sensing this expanded realm.

7. Breathe your angel's love into your heart. Breathe your angel's love into all your inner organs. Feel it beaming into your bones, glowing its way into all of your cells. Let your mind and your thoughts and your feelings be open to your angel's love for you, just as you are right now.

8. If you are looking for guidance, this is a wonderful opportunity to open to your angel. Ask for its expanded perceptions to weave their way into your own. Let yourself receive any images, thoughts, feelings, suggestions, that your angel beams out to you.

9. When you are filled with love and ready to move on, let your angel know. Then, feeling your aliveness, let your heart overflow with the joy of who you are and beam out that joy to your angel, as your way of thanking it. Soon, your angel's light will begin to fade, as it shifts its focus away from the physical dimensions. But know that it is still present, always present, just beyond the range of your physical senses.

10. Touch your physical body. Know that your consciousness is focused in your body, that you are fully grounded in the world, and yet able to encounter angels.

11. Feel your breath. Open your eyes if you have had them closed. Notice the room, the world, and as you do, shake out your body, wiggle, get up and move around. Feel the golden angel light still in you, as you move about your house. Know that you are bridging two realms as you move. Rejoice in this, that you are anchoring angel love in your body and in the world.

Each time you do this, you will be aligning yourself a little bit more with the angelic realm and allowing the angels to attune themselves a little more with the human realm. Doing this will awaken your body to joy. It will allow you to be more present in your body and more present in the world. It will support you in knowing why you are here and what you want to do for yourself and for the world. And it will strengthen your capacity to do what you decide to do.

▼▼▼▼▼▼▼▼▼▼▼▼▼▼▼▼▼▼▼▼▼▼▼▼▼

Suggestions for Living in the World

▲▲▲▲▲▲▲▲▲▲▲▲▲▲▲▲▲▲▲▲▲▲▲▲▲

1. At the end of this era in your history, the best way to live in the present is to act as if you were living in the future. The future shimmers with angels. The future shimmers with possibilities that you can help to manifest.

2. The United States has four percent of the population of the planet, but consumes over thirty percent of its resources. Use what is appropriate for your numbers. Give away excess possessions, share what you already have, use only recyclable and eco-balanced products. Live simply. Do not buy things that break. If you want something new, give something away. Angels have no possessions but our own natures. As you evolve, you, too, will own only what you can carry in your souls. Angels have no clothing. Our wings are garments of light. As you evolve you, too, will be clothed in light.

3. Water is life, and in the future it will become an increasingly valuable treasure. Not only must you learn to cut back on your use of water, but you must learn to keep it as clean as possible. Consider all the things you put into water. The cleansers you use for your homes, your clothing, and your bodies are toxic. You can clean everything with simple mixtures—water and vinegar for instance. Live fluidly, as angels do. Honor your beauty just as you are, without using colorings or clothes to redesign yourself. Let the ripples of your life be clean and pure. Leave the world as you found it, or more beautiful.

4. Trees are the lungs of your planet. Plant trees wherever you can.

More than any other embodied life-form on this planet, humans and angels resemble the trees, able to link Earth and Heaven. Plant seeds, plant trees, revivify the natural habitats that you have swept away. The planet itself is ready to work with you. The reforesting of your world can happen in less time than you imagine. In a circle of trees you will find the faith of angels calling.

5. You have legislated a minimum wage. Now it is time to think about a maximum wage, the amount of money that will allow you to take care of yourself and supply your basic needs in a balanced and integrated way. Find out what that amount is for yourself and give away everything you earn above that amount. Angels are fed by the universe itself. The four forces of nature that pour through us are all that we need.

6. Know that in everything you do, in everything you say, in everything you think, you make a difference in the world. Know that you and your angel are all that it takes to make dreams happen. Know that you are the answer. Celebrate.

▼▼▼▼▼▼▼▼▼▼▼▼▼▼▼▼▼▼▼▼▼▼▼▼▼▼▼▼

Talking to Your Body about Healing

▲▲▲▲▲▲▲▲▲▲▲▲▲▲▲▲▲▲▲▲▲▲▲▲▲▲▲▲

Your body is wise. It is also quite simple. Information is stored in every part of the body. The brain may be the focus and organizer of the nervous system, the information system, but it is not separate from the nerves. It would be far more useful to think of your consciousness as extending into every part of your body through your nerves, rather than being isolated in your head. Doing this will facilitate the healing process by allowing yourself to know that you are a conscious body, not just a conscious head.

Your body is conscious. It carries all of the memories of your life. If you fell and hit your head many years ago, and you did nothing to release the pain and fear and anger caused by that fall, your body still carries that information. But when you allow yourself to go back and feel the feelings, you can release them, no matter how many years have gone by.

Your body wants to heal. But in its simplicity, it does not know the difference between an event happening and an event being released. If you are ready to release the pain of hitting your head, when you go into your body and start to feel it, your body will react to it as if it were happening all over again, and the healing may not take. You may even doubt your ability to heal, because nothing changed.

But if you tell your body what is happening when you go into it and start to feel the pain again, if you talk to all your cells and tell them that you are releasing old pain, not experiencing it anew, then your body will release the memory instead of reacting to it. Rub your hands all over your body. Tell it with your hands and your thoughts and your words that you are about to release old patterns. When you are finished with the process, thank it for doing the releasing with you. This procedure is also helpful if you are going to a healer, an acupuncturist, or a surgeon.

When old energy is released by the body, empty spaces are created in the body's consciousness. Often, healing doesn't last because those spaces aren't filled in with new energy at the end of a healing session. Still carrying the memory of familiar pain, the body can easily draw back into itself new pain to fill the spaces. This, too, will corroborate the impression that healing doesn't work, that it is a mistake to feel old feelings. So at the end of a healing session, always take time to repattern the body. Feel joy in the areas that were cleansed. Feel light and ease and pleasure there. Touch your body, talk to your cells. Tell them that they are clear now and support them in repatterning themselves into wellness.

▼▼▼▼▼▼▼▼▼▼▼▼▼▼▼▼▼▼▼▼▼▼▼▼▼▼▼

Simple Tools for Co-creation

▲▲▲▲▲▲▲▲▲▲▲▲▲▲▲▲▲▲▲▲▲▲▲▲▲▲▲▲▲

In the journey toward understanding the nature of the physical, you may have thought that you were totally separate from God. That is not possible, as everything comes from God. In the past, every group of people had its different ways of connecting with God, in art, in dance, in scripture, in healing. Honor the ancient tools, for they will keep strong the roots of who you are as a species. And invent new ways to awaken yourselves to why you were born.

Participate in creation by becoming creators yourselves. You do not need paints or canvas. A song you sing is a tool for awakening. You do not need clay or wood to carve. A well-crafted story is a tool for awakening. You do not need a piano or guitar. A dance done with joy is a tool for awakening.

Every one of you is a creator in the midst of Creation. When you align with your soul, when you attune as we angels do, then you are awakened to God in your body, and you are ready to fulfill God's dreams in creating you.

▼▼▼▼▼▼▼▼▼▼▼▼▼▼▼▼▼▼▼▼▼▼▼▼▼▼

Food for Body and Soul

▲▲▲▲▲▲▲▲▲▲▲▲▲▲▲▲▲▲▲▲▲▲▲▲▲▲

Just because you were born doesn't mean that you are alive. Just because you are moving around in the world doesn't mean that you are awake.

Touch yourself all over. Feel the capacity for life in every cell. Nurture that capacity. Your attention will enliven you, awaken you. That is all that you need to do right now.

When your cells are alive and awake, they will open naturally and easily to love and joy, to ecstasy and bliss. You won't have to do a thing. Everything will take care of itself. And your life will work in all the ways you've dreamed of. No—it will work better, for you won't be dreaming anymore, you'll be living.

Your scientists tell you that within two years, every single cell in your entire body will be replaced by new cells. If that is true, then why do old imbalances remain? Why do illnesses continue? They continue because the stories you tell yourself are the same, because the patterns in the energy of your body remain the same. But if you tell new stories, and if you breathe your soul into your cells, then everything will change in your bodies.

The building blocks for new cells come from the food you eat. Be attentive to what you put in your body, to where it comes from, to what is in it, to how it is grown. Your body is brilliant, but it is also simple. It cannot handle the manufactured chemicals you put in it. The food that you eat may be plentiful, but if the soil is depleted, the water polluted, it cannot recreate you as you want.

Feel your soul energizing your body. Hold your hands above your food. Know that you can draw energy out from the core of your soul into your hands and then beam it into your food, to revivify it, to tune it to your particular body. Do this till you feel the energy you put into the food bouncing back into your hands. In this way, the building blocks of the new you will be alive, awake, and a blessing to your body.

▼▼▼▼▼▼▼▼▼▼▼▼▼▼▼▼▼▼▼▼▼▼▼▼▼▼▼

Living as a Liquid Body

▲▲▲▲▲▲▲▲▲▲▲▲▲▲▲▲▲▲▲▲▲▲▲▲▲▲▲

You may think that your world is solid, rigid, and cannot change. You may think that your society is rigid, dense, and cannot change. You may think that your body and your mind are dense and changeless on every level. But please remember that the axis of your planet is moving all the time, and that most of the surface of your world is liquid, and that your body is sixty to seventy percent liquid itself. And liquid changes. Easily.

If liquid changes easily, and you are mostly liquid, then you can change far more easily than you thought, and so can the cultures you human beings have created for yourselves. Blockages in your minds and bodies that seem permanent when you think of yourself as solid can shift and flow and change again when you remember your true state.

If you have access to a warm and quiet pool, go there. If you do not, you can do this on your bed or on the floor, preferably on a soft surface. Piles of many pillows would be excellent.

Lie on your back in the water, on the floor or bed, or on a sea of pillows. Feel your breath and notice anywhere that you are holding tension. See if you can release some of it by focusing on it, acknowledging it, and then exhaling it out of you. Let yourself relax. If you want to play soft music in the background, use something that is continuously fluid. Wave sounds would be ideal.

Feel your body. Let yourself be weightless. Tune your senses inward and feel the way that you are mostly water. Your blood is water, your cells are filled with water. Sensuously, feel your body all over, slowly and gently. As you touch yourself, be conscious of the fact that your fingers are mostly water and that what they are touching is mostly water too.

Now focus on any thoughts or any feelings in your body that you want to release. Feel your way into them with the same fluidity that you have been feeling in your body. Know that everything about you is liquid, that your brain is mostly water, and invite the same fluidity to enter your consciousness. As you do, new perceptions, new attitudes, new understandings, will flow into you easily and awaken you to harmony and healing.

Sense the world beneath you, whose food and energy gave birth to your body. Feel the way the planet itself shifts and changes, wobbles on its axis, dances. Dance with it. Move with it. Be one with it in its own great changes.

Do this exercise whenever you feel rigid or stuck, in yourself, in your relationships with others, or in your relationship with the world.

**Your Home
Is a Temple**

A temple is a place where energy is stored. Your home is a temple. What do you store there? What permeates the walls, furniture, the food you eat? What currents fill the air?

Is your home a place of anger, fear, or sorrow? Is your home a place of anxiety, depression, or despair? Whatever you are feeling, those energies are stored in your home. Whenever you come back to it, that is what fills you.

Explore all the rooms in your home. Sit in all the furniture. Open all the closets, all the cabinets. As you are exploring your home, feel all the feelings that are stored there. Tell the truth about what you find. Invite everyone in your household to do this, not as a way of proving anything or blaming anyone or making a point. Explore the feelings in your home so that you can heal them. Sit together and share what you have felt.

In the old days, every dwelling place had a hearth, a central place where the home fires kept burning. Today your hearth may not be your fireplace. Move through your home again and feel where the central place is for you. It is the kitchen for some, the bedroom for others—the garage, the bathroom, the garden, wherever. Sit in the hearth of your home and feel everything that is there, and then ask yourself what you want to feel in your home.

Know that what you want to feel is already in you, no matter how far away it seems. Open all the doors and windows. Let a fresh wind blow in. Know that all of your angels are working with you now to clean out the old energies of your home.

As you sit in your hearth space, feel the feelings you want to feel rippling out from you, into the walls, the floors, the ceilings. Feel them rippling out into the furniture. Do this every day, and every day that you do you will find the new feelings getting stronger and stronger.

Your home is a temple. Feel it tingling with love, joy, ecstasy, and bliss. Know that when you do this, each time that you come home, you bathe yourself in these energies, and they enter not just your sofa but your cells. Know that anyone who enters your home will also be healed by the energies you have generated.

Your home is a temple. A temple is an energy storage place. When you work with the energies of God, your home will be a holy place for you, your plants, your pets, your family, your friends, and the angels.

Laughter Is God's Blessing for Your Body

Put your hands on your heart and know that it is holy. Put your hands on your heart and feel the way that love, joy, ecstasy, and bliss are beaming in and out of it. Put your hands on your heart and know that the light of God's creation shines there. Put your hands on your heart and know that the dream of physicality that God created you to experience is possible now, in this time, for all of humanity.

Reach out your hands to each other in prayer. Pray with your bodies and sing. Reach out your hands to each other in hope: dance in hope, dance with joy, dance with angels. Reach out your hands to the angels and pray. Let us pray, all together, as one family. Reach out your hands to the heavens and Earth. In this time, in this place, God is unfolding.

Open your cells to the holiness of who you are. In the wisdom of your cells is a holiness of their own. Feel that holiness. And dance the dance of bodies that best aligns, attunes, and awakens. Laugh! Let laughter wash through you. Laugh with each other. Laugh with the angels. In laughter your planet will be blessed.

▼▼▼▼▼▼▼▼▼▼▼▼▼▼▼▼▼▼▼▼▼▼▼▼▼▼▼

The Pleasures of Sharing Joy

▲▲▲▲▲▲▲▲▲▲▲▲▲▲▲▲▲▲▲▲▲▲▲▲▲▲▲

That you exist at all is a gift from God, who wanted there to be a universe, who wanted there to be a You. The universe continues to exist from moment to moment because of a continuous outflowing of beingness from the eternal heart of God. You continue to exist because of this same continuous outflowing.

There are many things that you can do to heal yourselves and your world. You can cultivate inner wisdom, you can awaken yourselves to all that you were born to be. But the most delightful thing of all that you can do, to transform yourselves and your world, is to begin to explore the delicious pleasures of sharing joy.

You know the pleasures of sharing love, of sharing many of the different kinds of love. But just as there are 137 different colors in the spectrum of love, there are 228 different notes in the harmonics of joy.

Whenever you share joy, all of creation is affirmed. Whenever you share joy, you resonate in all your beingness with the patterns of your world. There is nothing so delicious, so pleasing, as the sharing of joy. When you are filled with joy, moving through the world as a joy-body, a nod, a smile, a word of thanks, a helping hand, given or received, awakens everyone's capacity to be human in the most enlivening way.

We angels are beings of love. We enter your lives to share love. Step out into the world today as the beings of joy that you are. Joy is a primal energy that permeates the universe. Celebrate who you are as beings of joy. Invite all of creation to celebrate with you.

You Now, Praying

Every atom is holy. Every atom is the center of the universe. Every cell is holy. Every cell is the center of who you are. You, now, alive and holy, you are the center of the universe. What can you do when you know that? What can you be when you know that angels circle around you, cheering you on?

You now, alive and holy, you are the center of all dreams. The universe began in dreams. Atoms rise up from dreams. You who are dream, who are atom, who are cell, who are holy, who are present, who stand living at the center, You are who you are waiting for. You are who God created You to be.

Thoughts shimmer. Feelings race. The forces of the universe—bliss, ecstasy, joy, and love—pour through your soul, immortal, and through your body, your holy body. Touch your body all over. Feel the life-force sweep through you. Let it pour forth in gratitude to God, the Unified Field, Ahanah, the Divine Parent of us all, of angels and humans and all that is. Let it pour forth in laughter.

This is prayer. This is the prayer that a body fully awakened to joy prays, alive and holy, unfolding with all of the universe.

AFTERWORD

For thousands of years you have learned from suffering and pain. Now you are ready to learn from love and joy instead. Now is the time when all of humanity can come together to create Heaven on Earth. Everyone who is alive now is a part of the transformation. Everyone who is alive now is needed in the transformation. Every moment is another opportunity to awaken.

The path is simple. The journey is easy. All the wisdom you need is already inside you. And when you open to the angels, all of your dreams will be possible. All the wounds of your lives and your world can be healed, in less time than you could ever have dreamed of.

Imagine a world where families and communities come together in love and are defined by love, all 137 different kinds.

Imagine a world where all work is done in joy, all 228 different kinds of joy, and done by people who are living in their joy-bodies, moving with the joyous body of your world.

Imagine a world where in schools, businesses, offices, governments, people begin each day by aligning with the angels, so that everything they do is co-created. See this happening at every level, with doctors, executives, scientists, and politicians all participating, and know that your imagining and your actions are helping to create this new world.

Imagine a world where borders and divisions are as fluid as water, where all of you honor your differences, at the same time as you celebrate your shared humanness. Imagine and participate in creating a world where all the different peoples of the world live in peace, sharing equally all the fruits of the Earth.

Imagine a world where all plants and animals are honored for being a part of the vital fabric of reality and are living in freedom. Together with the angels, you will be able to create healing for the air, the trees, the water, the earth, and for all the living beings on your world. The science of spirituality is the door to every kind of healing. When humans and angels hold the key together, we can open that door to change.

The journey begins with your own transformation. Let your mind and body remember and reexperience the joys that you have known. Each time you do this, you allow your cells to take in more joy. Touch yourself all over and say, "I am a being of joy."

As you heal and grow, the people around you will feel the possibilities for change within themselves, and they, too, will grow.

With mind and feelings and body filled with the light of your souls, everything is possible. Stand tall and know that you are a cousin to the angels. Stand tall and let the beauty of who you are shine out into the world. We are beings of love, and you are becoming beings of joy. Together we can change history. Together we *are* changing history.

Together we are creating that moment in the eternal present that you call—the future.

▼▼▼▼▼▼▼▼▼▼▼▼▼▼▼▼▼▼▼▼▼▼▼▼▼▼▼▼

Dancing into the Future

▲▲▲▲▲▲▲▲▲▲▲▲▲▲▲▲▲▲▲▲▲▲▲▲▲▲▲▲

The following exercise is a simple one designed to support your movement into the future. You can do it alone or with others. All that you need is the space and time to do it. Play some quiet healing music in the background if you like, but you may want to imagine the music.

1. Stand with your eyes closed and sense your body, posture, and the space around you.
2. Tune into your breathing, and as you inhale and exhale, let those movements begin to spread through your entire body. Let the breath be a wave that washes through you from head to toe, so that you are gently rocking and swaying.
3. Invite your angel in to join you. Feel it gathering itself in front of you, luminous and beautiful. Feel its wings stretched out toward you—children of Ahanah—both of you.
4. The sense of your angel is strong now. Touch the tips of your fingers to the tips of its wings. A golden current will begin to pass through you. The two of you begin to dance together, slowly, wing tips to fingertips, swaying with the music.
5. Feel the place that you are standing in. There are no walls

there. There are no limits to it. It is vast and open, and so are you. You are growing into this space. Invite the people that you love into this space and see them dancing with their angels too. Then invite neighbors, acquaintances, even world leaders, and see them all dancing with their angels to the same sweet music.

6. You realize now that this isn't a vast room that you are dancing in. It is the world. You can see everyone dancing together in joy, both those you call friends and those that you have called your enemies, whoever they are. This gathering is a grand re-union, a great party. Humans and angels—who came into be-ing together and went on separate journeys—are gathering together again, to share what we have learned.

7. Feel how you and your angel move in this dance. See the way that everyone else is dancing with their angels. Allow feelings to rise, images, choices. See and feel and hear yourself moving into a future in which you are fully alive, whole, and joyous, you and all of humanity. Notice where you are going, what you are doing, and who you are doing it with. Breathe all of this in, and know that you are making it possible as you dance.

8. Slowly, when you are ready, bring yourself back to the room you are in. Feel your connection to the Earth and the heavens. Feel your angel still with you. Thank it for the dance, and bring yourself fully back to the room. Know that this dance into to-morrow is seeding the future, for yourself, for all of humanity, and for all of the angels. Take the feelings and images with

you, as seeds, as inspiration, to nurture you through the days to come.

Go in peace. Peace is another name for joy. Be joy. That is your destiny. You are creating Heaven on Earth. You are creating it now. In joy you are creating it. Welcome to the future.

The Beginning

Andrew's
Acknowledgments

This book exists because of all the angels in my life, starting with my agent Howard Morhaim and my editor, Emily Bestler, whose clarity and enthusiasm have been such gifts. Also, their assistants, Alison Mullen and Amelia Sheldon, and a host of relatives and friends all supported me in this journey: Gerry Shields, Richard Ramer, Kate Shepherd, Steve Zipperstein, Michael Friedman, Chris Beach, Joy Manesiotis, Carol Robin, Bonnie Gintis, Cheryl Woodruff, Alma Daniel, Timothy Wyllie, Mindy Yanish, Cathy Deutsch, Avery Luna, Linda Leahy, Rob Leahy, Rita Maloney, Anne Walsh, Maryanne Quinones, Don Shewey, David Vincent, John Stowe, Prue See, Samuel Kirschner, Jeff Wadlington, Nelson Bloncourt, Marty Spiegel, Jeanne Barrett, Steve Sisgold, Carista Luminere, Kathlyn Hendricks, Gay Hendricks, Judith Burwell, Betsy Cochran, Will Paulsen, David Michaels, Ona Sachs, Leslie Windham, Diane Richardson, Andi Scott, Julia Berkhout, Steven Sashen, Rod Wells, Mark Horn, Leonard Ruder, Susan Snowe, Gerald Cohen, Michele Whitman. And Virginia Pugliese, Pamela Brennan, and everyone at Mail Boxes Etc. Carlotta, my beloved computer; Karen Haughey, for the beautiful image that graces the cover of this book; and Randy Lee Higgins, the companion of my life, who also dances with angels.

SARGOLAIS'S ACKNOWLEDGMENTS

Although the words of this book came through me, they were created by a collective of angels too numerous to name, but worthy of mention, amongst them *your* companion in the heavenly realms of liquid space and time.